# Teach from Your Best Self

Teachers, this book is a guide for taking care of education's most valuable resource: you. Author Jay Schroder, founder of the popular Teach from Your Best Self Institute, demonstrates why the version of ourselves that we bring to teaching matters and describes how we can rejuvenate ourselves while maximizing student learning. Part I explains why the self that a teacher brings to the classroom is important. Part II explores skills that will help us sustain a best-self state in all manner of situations. Part III delves into those moments when we're provoked beyond our limits and our "hurtspots" come sharply into view. It offers ways to avert a reactive state or recover from it. Lastly, Part IV provides simple approaches for building a more durable, best self for the long term—a best self with deepened capacity to respond rather than react in the pressurized conditions of teaching. With fresh ideas presented throughout, you'll learn how to prioritize your own well-being so you can continue to make a difference for your students.

**Jay Schroder** has taught high school English and social studies for the past twenty-four years in both mainstream and alternative education settings. In 2021, he founded the Teach from Your Best Self Institute, an organization with a mission to support and inspire educators while advancing a new model for revitalizing education.

T0386433

# Teach from Your Best Self

## A Teacher's Guide to Thriving in the Classroom

Jay Schroder

Routledge
Taylor & Francis Group

NEW YORK AND LONDON

First published 2024
by Routledge
605 Third Avenue, New York, NY 10158

and by Routledge
4 Park Square, Milton Park, Abingdon, Oxon, OX14 4RN

*Routledge is an imprint of the Taylor & Francis Group, an informa business*

*Library of Congress Cataloging-in-Publication Data*
Names: Schroder, Jay, author.
Title: Teach from your best self : a teacher's guide for thriving in the classroom / Jay Schroder.
Description: New York : Routledge, 2024. | Includes bibliographical references. |
Identifiers: LCCN 2023005253 | ISBN 9781032419435 (hbk) | ISBN 9781032416878 (pbk) | ISBN 9781003360513 (ebk)
Subjects: LCSH: Teaching--Psychology--Handbooks, manuals, etc. | Effective teaching. | Teachers--Psychology. | Teachers--Attitudes. | Teachers--Job stress--Prevention. | Stress management. | Well-being. | Educational change.
Classification: LCC LB1025.3 .S394 2024 | DDC 371.102--dc23/eng/20230329
LC record available at https://lccn.loc.gov/2023005253

ISBN: 978-1-032-41943-5 (hbk)
ISBN: 978-1-032-41687-8 (pbk)
ISBN: 978-1-003-36051-3 (ebk)

DOI: 10.4324/9781003360513

Typeset in Palatino
by SPi Technologies India Pvt Ltd (Straive)

*This book is dedicated to my mentor, Paul Richards, who continues to inspire, challenge, and believe in me.*

*And it's dedicated to the educators who endure heartbreaking conditions in education to give kids a shot at a great life. You are my heroes.*

# Contents

.

# Introduction

This is a book for teachers. Unlike most education books, this book puts you, the teacher, at the center. It's a guide for taking care of education's most valuable resource, which is you.

Every successful organization has a source of magic. Corporations go to great lengths to protect this—the formula for Coca-Cola, Colonel Sanders's secret recipe. Think of that source of magic as the goose that lays the golden eggs for the organization. Organizations fail when they don't take care of their golden-egg-laying geese.

In education, the goose is not the textbook, it's not the technology, it's not the curriculum, and it's definitely not the standardized test. It's not even the students. If you put 30 students in a room by themselves and supply that room with textbooks, computers, and learning materials, it's unlikely that anything resembling constructive learning will occur until you bring in a teacher. For decades, education has been abusing and neglecting its golden-egg-laying geese, and now the whole system is on the verge of collapse.

Even before the Covid-19 pandemic had stretched many educators beyond the breaking point, 44% of teachers were leaving the profession during their first five years on the job (*Richard Ingersoll Updates*, 2018). The stresses of teaching during the pandemic and in the aftermath have made the situation worse. According to a May 2021 report from the CDC Foundation, 27% of teachers self-reported symptoms consistent with clinical depression, 37% of teachers self-reported symptoms consistent with generalized anxiety, and 53% of teachers reported that they are considering quitting (*Mental Health Impact*, 2021). A subsequent survey conducted by the National Education Association and published in early 2022 showed that since the onset of the pandemic, "55% of

DOI: 10.4324/9781003360513-1

educators are thinking about leaving the profession earlier than they had planned" (Walker, 2022).

So many teachers have been leaving that there aren't enough qualified teacher applicants to replace them, causing staffing shortages in districts throughout the nation (Lieberman, 2021). School administrators have been coping with tens of thousands of unfilled positions by expanding class sizes and having teachers spend their prep periods substituting in other classes, creating even more stress for the teachers who remain. Some states have dealt with the problem by lowering standards for who can teach, filling positions with people who are ill prepared for the realities of the classroom.

For decades, teachers have been treated like replaceable cogs in a student-processing machine, as if teacher turnover didn't matter. But teacher turnover matters. A 2012 study of 850,000 fourth- and fifth-grade students over eight academic years in New York City found that teacher turnover harms student learning (Ronfeldt et al., 2013). It's also expensive. A 2017 study showed that districts spend more than $20,000 every time a teacher leaves (*What's the Cost of Teacher Turnover*, 2017). Nationally, that's an annual cost to school districts of $8 billion (Garcia & Weiss, 2019).

It's no wonder teachers are leaving. Teachers make on average 20% less than other professionals with similar education and experience (Allegeretto & Mishel, 2020). They are assigned large classes of students with widely varying skill levels, many of whom have no interest in learning what the teacher is assigned to teach them. Some students enter the classroom impacted by trauma or social pathologies that poorly equip them to learn anything at all. Schools are dealing with a surge of mental health issues to such an extent that the American Academy of Child and Adolescent Psychiatry and the Children's Hospital Association "declared the pandemic-related decline in child and adolescent mental health a national emergency" (Vestal, 2021). Meanwhile, opportunistic outside forces are seizing on the crisis to interfere with the work teachers do while beating a steady drum of misinformation that adds to the chaos and villainizes educators.

These are the circumstances in which classroom teachers struggle to help students close pandemic-caused learning gaps, while trying to avoid getting Covid and worrying about protecting their students and themselves from getting shot. This convergence of troubles has led public education into "a crisis of epic proportions" (Meckler, 2022; Perna, 2022), with a recent survey naming teachers the most burned-out employees in America (Marken & Agrawal, 2022).

Since the report *A Nation at Risk* was published in 1983, education reform has been focused on standards, rigorous testing, and a succession of new initiatives for teachers to implement. Though not given a voice in these reforms, the burden of carrying out the initiatives and the responsibility of ensuring their success has fallen to teachers. When students fail to meet the desired results on standardized tests, new mandates are instituted that require teachers to learn new strategies, new techniques, new instructional methods, new technology, all of which teachers are expected to implement under conditions of ever tighter oversight and control.

This myopic focus on making teachers do more and controlling what they do is based on the false notion that if teachers could just do enough of the right things, then test scores would increase, classes would run smoothly, and schools would finally be successful. Having been told for the past 23 years that I must learn to do more kinds of classroom cartwheels to improve student learning, it's clear to me that this is a road to nowhere. Even before the pandemic, in spite of the billions of dollars spent and untold teacher hours devoted, educational outcomes had flatlined or declined. Trends in national data show that twelfth-grade math skills in 2019 were the same as in 2005, while reading skills in 2019 dropped seven points compared with 1992 (National Assessment of Educational Progress, 2019).

It's hardly surprising that student performance isn't increasing. The cost of requiring teachers to do more and more is increased teacher stress. Studies show that teacher stress and burnout negatively affect student performance, essentially subverting the gains one might expect from teachers' additional work. The first empirical study of the relationship between the emotional exhaustion of teachers and student achievement was conducted in Germany in 2016 and involved 1,102 German elementary school students. This study was designed to explore the association between teacher stress and student performance in mathematics. Controlling for factors such as the teacher's gender and years of experience, as well as the students' socio-economic status and cognitive abilities, researchers discovered that teachers' emotional exhaustion correlated with significantly lower student mathematics achievement. The negative effect of teacher stress on student performance was higher in classes containing greater numbers of language-minority students (Klusmann et al., 2016).

Clearly, education needs an approach that prioritizes the well-being of teachers. One starting place is to consider the way of the *ninja*. In feudal Japan, the ninja were stealthy fighters who specialized in covert missions. Ninja missions were often harrowing, and the ninja were always outnumbered; however, the ninja were so good at what they did, they inspired legends. The way of the ninja was *in shin tonkei*, which means creating the greatest effect with the least amount of effort. *In shin tonkei* required that the ninja know in every situation what mattered most and concentrate their efforts there.

After over two decades of waging my own covert mission to find a sustainable approach to teaching, I have discovered that what matters most isn't what I *do*. It's not the strategies I use, the standards I teach to, the technology I utilize, or the instructional methods I employ. It's the quality of my presence, the state of being I bring to my students.

Teachers already have a sense that the quality of their presence matters. When they're having an off day, when they're flustered or stressed out, things don't go as well regardless of the strength of their lesson plans. But when they step in front of their students open and refreshed, just about any decent teaching strategy is likely to work.

The influence that a teacher's state of being has on students is both profound and ignored. In the high-stress conditions of education, a teacher tends to teach from whatever version of themselves the circumstances bring out. For instance, having too much to do and not enough time to do it is likely to bring out a version of the teacher that is overwhelmed and maybe irritable.

People assume they are stuck with whatever version of themselves circumstances stir up—that it's natural to react to chaotic, stressful situations with a grumpy, agitated self. But this is not so. We are never stuck with any version of ourselves. In the wings of every moment, there is a best self quietly waiting to be chosen and embodied to help us meet each circumstance in our own best way.

By "best self," I don't mean a state of continuous composure. Rather, I am suggesting that we are at our best when we are the most authentic—when we are connected to our deepest values, open and curious, able to respond to the situation rather than react. As we learn to access this best self and act from it, our teaching transforms. Our students learn, and we are fulfilled in our work.

As it exists right now, the education system is not built to support teachers to bring their best. However, once enough of us are conserving ourselves and beginning to thrive, we can use our joined voices to turn schools into communities of learning that support the best self of every teacher, learner, school employee, administrator, parent, and volunteer who steps into the building.

The first step in enacting this change is to give teachers classroom approaches they can begin implementing today that will increase their effectiveness and help them preserve their well-being. The purpose of this book is to hand you methods so that, no matter the culture of your school—the policies, the circumstances, the mandates—you can, ninjalike, employ *in shin tonkei* to achieve high-impact teaching with less effort.

## The Experiences and Influences Behind This Book

This book would not be possible if it weren't for three powerful forces in my life: an illness, a mentor, and a karate path.

Chronic illness is rarely considered to be positive; however, it can force us to learn things we would otherwise never learn. During my final semester of college, I succumbed to chronic fatigue syndrome. After staggering my way to graduation—right when my adult life was supposed to be starting—I moved back in with my parents and went to bed for a year. During this period, I saw a parade of doctors, none of whom were able to help. I spent much of my twenties depressed or asleep.

I didn't begin to recover until I stopped fighting my health condition and started to accept it. This was neither easy nor intuitive. My health improved enough for me to go back to school to earn a teaching credential. I became a teacher, but I was still far from healthy; the smallest bit of stress would flatten me. To survive as a teacher, I had to lower my stress and preserve my energy. But how? The daily pressures of teaching were overwhelming. There were plenty of days when, just to get through, I slept on the floor behind my desk during lunch, and plenty of weekends when I couldn't get out of bed. But over time, I developed approaches to teaching that left me fulfilled instead of wrecked. In time, I found that the approaches I used to conserve my health were not only good for me; they were good for my students as well.

I could not have learned any of this had I not been exposed to new perspectives from a mentor. In my early 30s, I landed in southern Oregon so broke that I had to sell my clunker car to rent an apartment. I bought a bicycle and got a job waiting tables. I heard from a friend about a man named Paul Richards who, I was told, could see things. I didn't know what to make of this, but I was eager to talk to anyone who might be able to help me with my health condition. We arranged to meet, and on a warm spring morning, I pedaled my bicycle to his house.

In the previous decade, I had met a lot of people who claimed to have some unique ability; most had been disappointments. I parked my bike, and Paul, smiling widely, stepped out of his front door to greet me. He shook my hand, and I followed him into his music studio, a small outbuilding where he kept his guitar, a computer, a keyboard, and a mixing console.

Paul casually explained that, as a young man, he'd been mentored and trained in specialized ways of using awareness and attention. If I decided to learn from him, he didn't want me to believe anything he said. Instead, he wanted me to experiment and test the skills out for myself. The best reason to learn, he said, his eyes twinkling, was because it was fun.

In that first conversation, Paul uncannily summed up two challenges I was facing. The first was that by living at the fringe of society without any kind of professional certification, I was doomed to struggle just to make ends meet. The second was that I believed too much in my own effort and that continuing to live that way would most certainly continue to drain me. I needed a career, and I needed a new approach to life.

I began meeting with Paul regularly. One day, he gave me a laminated card to put in my billfold. On one side were the words "Question Your Instincts." On the other side, "Trust Your Presence." I carry this card as a reminder that my instinctual reactions to situations, many of which bring up my worst self, always lead to the same old outcomes I've experienced a thousand times before. But an open, curious presence—a best self, in other words—opens the door for new experiences and much richer returns.

Paul was a black belt in karate, and after working with me for a few months, he suggested I take up karate as well. Over the past two decades, I've trained under two karate senseis. I earned my black belt from Sensei Aaron Ortega. After Sensei Aaron retired from teaching karate, I began training with Grandmaster Tom Spellman. Both men have profoundly shaped my development as a martial artist and as a man. While Sensei Aaron gave me the basics, expertly modeling the mindset of a warrior, Sensei Spellman refined my technique, introduced me to the history of martial arts, and taught me how I could use martial arts principles to improve my whole life.

Although neither Paul nor either of my karate senseis focused on helping me become a better teacher, my illness galvanized me to hear everything they offered through the lens of how I could teach without destroying my health. In 2000, as a second-year teacher, I told the principal's secretary that I was going to learn how to do this job in a way that filled me up rather than depleted me. At the time, I had no idea how to do this.

It took me 15 years, and a great deal of struggle along the way, to fulfill that promise, but I did. In 2018, my father passed away, and I started thinking about my own limited time. I knew

I had something valuable to share with other teachers, so I spent the next year developing material for a teacher training. Then the pandemic hit and trainings stopped, so I pivoted to writing this book.

In 2021, I led the first Teach from Your Best Self training—designed as a full-year experience that started with a one-week intensive workshop followed by monthly Saturday sessions. I wanted to know if what I had learned was shareable, if it could benefit other teachers as it had benefited me. And if indeed it benefited other teachers, I wanted to know if those benefits would flow toward their students. It turned out that the training worked; the participants were unanimous in that this material needed to be shared as widely as possible.

## About This Book and How to Use It

This book draws on my own experience as well as research in neuroscience, psychology, trauma research, Eastern martial arts systems, and other traditions. It is organized in four parts, and I recommend reading them sequentially.

In Part I, "The Challenge of Teaching," we tour through the obstacles, often misidentified, that teachers face and explore why the self that a teacher teaches from matters so much.

In Part II, "Skills and Principles That Matter," we explore practical classroom approaches for sustaining a best-self state in all manner of classroom situations. In addition, we explore how teachers can inspire students to be in their own best self, which makes the teacher's job immensely easier.

In Part III, "Tools for Emotionally Challenging Moments," we delve into those moments when we're provoked beyond our limits. We look at research-backed approaches for averting a reactive state and, if we do fall from our best self, recovering it as quickly as possible.

In Part IV, "Creating a Resilient Best Self," we consider research-supported ways of dismantling the psychological machinery that, when triggered, hijacks us from our best self. In this part of the book I introduce simple, time-efficient approaches for building a more resilient best self, one with deepened capacity to handle the pressure-filled conditions of teaching.

Finally, in the Conclusion, we consider how the Teach from Your Best Self model can be used to transform education.

At the end of each chapter you'll see instructions to grab pen and paper and respond to a few reflective questions. Reflecting on these questions in writing will help you to integrate the approaches introduced in each chapter into your daily teaching routine.

You may consider reading this book as part of a book group with other educators, discussing your responses to the reflective questions when you meet. To quote a line from poet William Stafford, "The darkness around us is deep," which is an apt description of the circumstances in which teachers perform society's most sacred task. Under such conditions, it helps to work together.

I'm honored to be your guide as we take this journey. So come on, let's go.

# Part I

## The Challenge of Teaching

# 1

# Attempting to Do an Impossible Job

I didn't always want to be a teacher. As a college student, I wanted to be a professor; I saw K-12 teachers as shabby distant cousins to my professors, who seemed worldly and cool. I imagined myself like them, wearing a tweed elbow-patched jacket and smoking a pipe in my book-filled office, then stepping into a lecture hall to deliver enthralling lectures. I dove hard into my studies, driving myself into frequent all-nighters. After two years of this, my body began to collapse. I drank more caffeinated soda and coffee to compensate until I was a jittery bag of exhaustion, increasingly wracked with headaches and mysterious digestive ailments. Eventually, I received the diagnosis of chronic fatigue syndrome, and that was the end of my dream of going on to graduate school to become a professor.

For the next decade, I floated from one dead-end job to the next, growing out my hair and taking buses and third-class trains into Mexico and Central America, where food was cheap and nobody cared if I slept all day under a tree. My wanderings took me to southern Oregon, where I met Paul Richards. I knew he was right about my needing a profession. By then it no longer made sense to go to graduate school for four more years to become a professor, so I enrolled in a teacher preparation program.

DOI: 10.4324/9781003360513-3

While studying to be a teacher, I spent a lot of time day-dreaming about what teaching would be like. Borrowing heavily from my romantic ideas about being a college professor, I saw myself holding forth while earnest students listened, enraptured. They would be so inspired by the discussions, their eager hands would fly into the air.

It took only a few minutes of actual teaching for that illusion to pop like a country fair balloon. My real-life students weren't interested in learning what I had to teach them. They would much rather talk to each other or mess around in class than do the lesson. I swung wildly between wanting them to like me and needing them to shut up and sit down. At the end of the day, when all my wires were fried, my sixth-period students rolled in, an all-star team of class clowns. Let's just say my classroom management skills weren't up to the task. I remember trying to get students to stop body surfing on the desks while I was attempting to teach "To Build a Fire," and the pandemonium in the middle of one class period when, during a storm, the electricity suddenly went out and the windowless classroom went completely black.

The only classroom management technique I had been taught during my teacher preparation program was to write misbehaving students' names on the chalkboard and add check marks to their names if they continued to misbehave. A trusted professor had shared this technique, and I had made a mental note to remember it. After my third day of failure as a teacher, I thought: *Okay, time to get serious.* The next day my students erupted into hilarity at their exasperated teacher furiously writing names and making check marks on the chalkboard.

I began falling into such despair that during my commute to work, which included a long stretch of straight road and a clear view of smoke billowing from a paper mill in the distance, the weirdly hopeful idea would leap unbidden into my mind that maybe the school was on fire and I could return home to my warm, comfortable bed.

What I didn't know at the time, because nobody ever said this to me, is that teaching is an insanely difficult job. It's so hard, it's virtually impossible. Not knowing this, I feared I was simply bad at it and needed to improve (which was also true). I assumed that my teacher preparation program had given me what I needed to succeed, so if the approaches and strategies I'd learned weren't working, the fault must lie with me. This drove me to stay late in the classroom trying to remedy my teaching deficiencies by writing "more engaging curriculum," while my wife (soon to be ex-wife) and baby daughter waited at home.

## Compulsory Education: Some Historical Context

Many people assume that low-achieving students tell the story of failing schools and failing teachers. This assumption over-looks the history of education and the fact that compulsory K-12 education is in fact a relatively recent idea. Compulsory educa-tion is actually a giant experiment, and we are still figuring out how best to do it.

For most of human history, skills and knowledge were passed from one generation to the next through the time-tested method of mentor/apprentice relationships. This is how our ancestors passed along the stuff that mattered, whether that was knowing what plants were edible, how to make a shelter or a hand ax, how to weave yarn into cloth, or how to plant and harvest.

With the advent of the Industrial Revolution and the recog-nition that great wealth could be created through cheap factory labor, the apprenticeship model waned, and public education, a model better suited for inuring people to perform the monoto-nous tasks required in factories, took its place. School got kids off the streets and effectively sorted the studious ones, who would go on to college, from the ones headed for the farms or the facto-ries. In addition, vast numbers of immigrants were coming to the United States, and America needed a common experience that would help initiate immigrant children into a shared national identity. For these original purposes, compulsory education worked. Elementary school became the common experience of every child, who learned to read, write, and perform basic arith-metic while being taught civic lessons about what it meant to be an American. Most students stopped attending by fourth or fifth grade to work on a farm or in a factory or to help with the chores at home. The ones who stuck around enrolled in college and became doctors, lawyers, scholars, and scientists.

America only gradually warmed to the idea of 12 years of compulsory schooling and a high school diploma for all. In 1900, a scant 6% of students finished high school (*U.S. High School Graduation Rates*, n.d.). In 1902, high school became more standardized, with 15 units (measured by seat time) required for graduation (Golden, 1998). High school graduation rates accelerated after 1910 as the US economy began creating greater numbers of white-collar jobs that demanded more formal education than the first eight grades provided. The Great Depression caused a flood of young people to enter high school as the jobs that had previously been plentiful for teens dried up. By 1940, 51% of students earned their high school diploma. About the midpoint of the twentieth century, high school began to be seen as preparing students for life rather than just for college, which prompted changes in curriculum. Rather than focusing solely on college preparation, new classes were brought in, ranging from metals to dressmaking. From the 1960s through 2011, the graduation rates vacillated between 60% and 80%.

It wasn't until the early 2000s that researchers started paying attention to graduation rates. At the time, about 70% of students were graduating from high school, meaning that about 30% were not. Politicians got on board, calling it a "drop-out crisis" and sounding the alarm to pass the No Child Left Behind Act. It was during this period that a high school diploma became the minimum standard for every student. Universal high school graduation was the goal, and graduation rates began to inch upward, finally cracking 80% in 2012 (Heckman & LaFontaine, 2010).

Never before in the history of human beings have we attempted to force entire generations through a 12-year process to learn things they don't care to learn. Struggling schools don't tell a story of failing teachers; they tell a story of a heroic class of professionals stepping up to do something that's never been done before.

## Effective Teaching May Be the Hardest Job There Is

In 2008, a reality television show debuted called *America's Toughest Jobs*. Contestants competed to perform a variety of difficult jobs, and their performance was rated by workers or employers in the respective fields. In the world of this show, America's toughest jobs included trucking in Alaska, crab fishing, and logging. Clearly, these are hard jobs. During my first two years of college, I worked summers and winter vacations on a logging crew. I know what it's like to be up at 4:00 in the morning to reach the logging site by 6:00 and spend the next ten hours running around on hillsides with a heavy cable and crawling on my belly, digging under logs to set the choker so the logs could be dragged to the landing. As tough as that job was, it wasn't remotely as tough as teaching. Here's why.

As William Glasser explains in his book *The Quality School: Managing Students Without Coercion*, every occupation falls into one of two categories: jobs managing (or performing an operation on) people and jobs managing (or performing an operation on) things (Glasser, 1990, pp. 15–25). As a choker-setter on a logging crew, I worked on things. As a teacher, I manage people. Jobs working on things offer a big advantage over jobs managing or performing an operation on people: things don't resist. A rusty bolt doesn't fight the mechanic's efforts, cussing him out as he attempts to loosen it. But when managing people, there is always the risk that the people one is trying to manage will resist and sabotage the process. This is why jobs that involve managing or performing an operation on people tend to have built-in ways to ensure cooperation. Surgeons put patients to sleep, which effectively turns them into things that can more easily be worked on. Managers fire insubordinate employees and replace them with ones who will cooperate. Platoon sergeants yell at recruits and make them do PT until they throw up and learn to follow orders. Notably, tools like these are not given to teachers.

Moreover, it's generally understood that if the person being managed through a process doesn't cooperate and the process fails, the blame falls on the uncooperative person, not the person managing them. When a patient ignores the doctor's orders and continues eating French fries and bacon-wrapped hot dogs and then dies of a heart attack, nobody blames the doctor. However, when students resist learning or don't do their best on standardized tests, the onus is often placed on the teacher.

Finally, in most jobs that involve managing or performing an operation on people, the person undergoing the process has volunteered for it, which goes a long way toward ensuring cooperation. We seek out a dentist to fix our teeth. We make the call if we want an Uber driver to take us somewhere. We sign up for a workshop and then open our wallets to pay for it. I can think of only five populations who are systematically put through a difficult process for which they did not volunteer: prisoners, people getting arrested, people conscripted into the military, severely mentally ill patients who are institutionalized, and K-12 students. With all these populations except the last, the person in charge is authorized to use force to compel cooperation. If you resist arrest, for instance, you will be tased, tackled, cuffed, and then arrested. Teachers are not given tasers to make students get off Snapchat and pay attention to the lesson. We are given smartboards and books and colored whiteboard markers.

Among all the jobs that involve managing or performing an operation on people, teaching is the only one with this unique combination of challenges: the teacher has no way to ensure cooperation; when students fail, the teacher is often blamed; and the students have not volunteered to learn what the teacher has been assigned to teach them. This perfect storm of obstacles makes effective teaching an insanely difficult job, perhaps the hardest job there is.

## The Scylla and Charybdis of Cynicism and Resignation

In Homer's *Odyssey*, to make his way home to Ithaca, Odysseus has to find a way to navigate through a narrow strait. On one side of the strait is Scylla, a six-headed, long-necked, man-eating monster who will surely snatch his men as Odysseus' ship rows by. On the other side of the strait is Charybdis, a monster who drinks and belches forth water. If Odysseus rows too close to Scylla, she will seize and devour his men, but if he rows too close to Charybdis, he will lose his entire ship, and he and his crew will drown. This is the kind of dilemma that teachers face: to have a long and fulfilling career, they must thread the needle between the forces of cynicism and resignation.

I first met the power of cynicism as a new teacher. Struggling and failing, I looked to the veteran teachers, hoping to learn how they managed to do this job year after year. Sitting in the staff lounge during lunch breaks, I listened closely for wisdom. Instead, the lunch conversation regularly revolved around complaining—about the administration, about school policies, but mostly about students. Although it was a joyless way to spend a lunch, as a new teacher I joined in. As I did, I discovered that the griping and grumbling offered a benefit. By blaming students, I could feel slightly better about my failures as a teacher—it wasn't me who was failing after all; it was my students. This seemed brilliant until I noticed the effect that blaming students had on me. I started feeling bitter. Although complaining about students enabled me to protect my self-esteem, the cost was my passion for teaching.

I didn't want to become the grumpy teacher, counting down the days to retirement. So I stopped having lunch in the staff lounge, and I stopped complaining about students. This, however, left me with my failures and no one to blame but myself. I began to feel the pull toward giving up.

Within a few years, contract negotiations between the district leadership and teachers began to sour. The president of the local union asked if I would speak at a school board meeting on behalf of the membership, and I agreed. My goal was to convince the board members not to increase demands on teachers who were already at the breaking point. As part of my preparation, I researched teacher retention: How many teachers leave the profession? Why do they leave? What does it cost school districts when teachers leave? I was astounded to learn that almost half of all teachers quit within the first five years of teaching.

That's when I realized that the two most likely outcomes for me were to become bitter and cynical, or to become demoralized and leave the profession. I didn't want to do either. I needed to find a way through this dilemma that would allow me to continue teaching while retaining whatever scraps of passion I could.

As for my speech, it fell on deaf ears. Within the year, we were on strike.

 **REFLECTION QUESTIONS**

*Grab a notebook and something to write with and respond to the following questions:*

1  What pressures and challenges do you face in your job?
2  How does this chapter's description of the difficulty of teaching affect your perception of your job and yourself as a teacher?
3  Despite the difficulty of teaching, what do you love about it?

# 2

# Learning to Teach from My Best Self

When I was a kid, one of the best things my parents did was to move to a house in the middle of five acres of forest. Whenever things got bad in the house, I would walk out the front door and into the trees. I would sit for hours on an old-growth log watching birds flit among the branches, inhaling the scents of cedar and decaying tree stumps. I learned something from that forest that would later help me as a teacher: I learned that different environments can evoke different versions of me. Back in the house, as my siblings and parents yelled at each other, I would become keyed up and anxious. But in the forest, my breathing slowed. I felt both calm and vividly alive. In the forest, I became someone I rather liked.

Early in my teaching career, there wasn't a day when I didn't experience the weight of chronic fatigue symptoms. I couldn't just override my condition—grab another cup of coffee and plow ahead. Whenever I tried that, I'd end up crashing for days. If I was going to make it in this profession, I had to find ways to conserve my energy, build up my reserves, and minimize the wear and tear of stress on my body. In short, I needed to learn to be that forest version of myself in the face of the pressure of teaching. For a long time this seemed impossible, but then, through karate, I learned that I could train myself to do it.

DOI: 10.4324/9781003360513-4

I started training in karate about the time I began teaching and was surprised by how much I loved it. I loved the smell of the dojo, the rustle and snap of the karate *gi* as I punched and kicked. Karate helped me connect to my body and made me feel more alive. On days when I felt too tired to train, I would get myself off the couch by recalling previous times I'd felt tired only to find that the training gave me more energy than it took. Going from a hectic day at school to the dojo was like walking out the front door of my childhood home into the forest. However, there was one aspect of karate training that wasn't relaxing: *kumite*.

*Kumite* is a training exercise that involves one person practicing defensive and counter techniques while another is punching, kicking, or otherwise attacking him. The ultimate version of *kumite* is free sparring, where both practitioners are attacking, trying to score points with kicks and punches that get through their opponent's defenses. In Sensei Aaron Ortega's dojo, free sparring was basically controlled fighting, where "controlled" meant trying not to send each other to the hospital. The idea was to throw medium-hard techniques to the body and light ones to the face, but as the adrenaline kicked in, keeping yourself and your opponent safe was like grabbing the tail of a dragon. We all got hurt. I frequently went home with a cracked rib or a bloody lip, but I loved it—an opponent's fist slamming into my face woke me up, bringing vivid clarity to the situation. Yet no matter how often Sensei Aaron told me to relax, I didn't know how to untense myself when larger, stronger men were punching and kicking me.

After training for seven years, Sensei Aaron thought that I and two other students were ready to test for black belt. As part of the test, he set up a 100-man *kumite*, a grueling ordeal in which we would each fight experienced black belts for 100 two-minute rounds.

Early on the morning of the test, the three of us black belt candidates, Sensei Aaron, and the black belts we would be fighting gathered in a local parking lot. We carpooled two hours into the wooded mountains of Northern California. At the end of a long, muddy driveway that wound through thick forest, we arrived at a cabin, a weathered structure that sat near a creek. Inside, a thin blue carpet stretched across the floor. An iron wood stove squatted at one end.

As we were warming up, Paul Richards, who was one of the black belts invited to the test, showed up and poked his head in the door. "Is this where the pansies are?" he joked.

After the demonstrations of kata and board breaking, the 100-man *kumite* began. At about round 50, I looked to my right and saw one of the other black belt candidates doubled over trying to catch his breath. His mouth was bleeding; his white karate *gi* was splattered with blood. On my left, the other candidate had large purple bruises swelling on his cheekbones. His feet were a mess—blistered on the bottom and bleeding from pivoting on the carpet. I was the smallest man in the room and, I think, the most beat up. The black belts' fists had been in my face all morning. I had just taken a shot on the chin that knocked me back against the wall. The muscles of my jaw locked up; I couldn't open my mouth. Still, we bowed once again to the black belts standing across from us and waited for the command to begin the next two-minute round.

About round 70, Sensei Aaron buried a side kick into my solar plexus that crumpled me, and I couldn't breathe. As soon as I caught my breath, I continued, fighting at the razor's edge between control and street fight. Meanwhile, I noticed that Paul, who was rotating through the rounds along with us, looked completely relaxed and seemed to be enjoying himself, smiling each time he sparred with me.

In round 99, one of the black belts hit me hard with a straight punch to my nose, which began gushing blood. As I was stuffing my nose with cotton and trying to catch my breath before the final round, Paul pulled me aside. He smiled as he watched me wipe blood off my face and said, "Jay, when you're sparring, what matters most isn't whether you hit someone or even evade their punches. What's most important is whether you can remain centered, clear, and responsive under the pressure of their attack." Then he added: "The secret of karate is learning how to stay centered and relaxed under pressure."

What Paul was saying is that my opponent and what he does matter less than my own state of being. From a state in which

I am centered, clear, and responsive—my best self, in other words—I can respond to any situation with the best I have, which is the most any of us can do. This was my introduction to what it means to spar from my best self. Instead of being tense and reactionary, from a relaxed, best-self state, I have access to all my karate skills—and, more important, to a responsive, improvised creativity about how to best use those skills in the moment.

This was a wild reorientation, and it came with big questions: How could I stop making not getting hit the most important thing? How could I keep my fear from making me tense and reactionary? Although I earned my black belt, that Saturday marked the beginning of my true karate training. Hilariously, I showed up to teach on Monday morning with three cracked ribs, a broken nose, and two black eyes.

The Japanese have a word for the state of mind Paul was referring to: *zanshin*. It's defined as a state of receptive awareness, undisturbed by circumstances, with a readiness to meet any situation. In the *zanshin* state, a person retains a kind of inner quietude even in stressful circumstances. The legendary Zen Swordmaster Takuan Soho described the essence of this state of mind:

> When the swordsman stands against his opponent, he is not to think of the opponent, nor of himself, nor of his enemy's sword movements. He just stands there with his sword which, forgetful of all technique, is ready only to follow the dictates of the subconscious. The man has effaced himself as the wielder of the sword. When he strikes, it is not the man but the sword in the hand of the man's subconscious that strikes.
>
> (Hyams, 1979)

Hungarian psychologist Mihaly Csikszentmihalyi popularized this state of mind in the West, calling it the flow state. In athletics, it is called being in the zone. Eastern traditions value this state and have developed processes, such as meditation, that help a practitioner build their capacity to retain *zanshin* while in action—whether that be performing a tea ceremony, practicing archery, doing calligraphy, training to fight, or, indeed, even while fighting for one's life. Martial arts folklore is built around the extraordinary things fighters have done from *zanshin*.

As I grew my ability to maintain *zanshin* under pressure in the dojo, I began changing as a teacher. Students started commenting on how much they liked coming to my class because the vibe was calm and relaxed. I stopped being reactionary when dealing with disruptive students. My classroom management issues dwindled, and I only rarely needed to write discipline referrals. In time, I didn't need to write them at all. No matter what my students did, I had relaxed access to all my teaching strategies and skills, plus an ongoing connection with my creativity to deal with any situation. I had found a way to teach with less effort, less stress. Teaching began to be fun.

I spent years using my classroom as a second training dojo, increasing my ability to maintain *zanshin* under pressure and experimenting with ways of lessening the pressure my students felt in school, which made them more open and receptive to learning. I started working in alternative education, teaching the most resistant students. The dean once asked me why I wasn't writing referrals like the other teachers. I wasn't sure how to answer; at the time, I didn't have an easy way to explain what I had been learning.

After witnessing my father's sad descent into Alzheimer's and subsequent death, I realized that if I had indeed discovered something worth sharing, I'd better share it while I still could. My sisters and I sold the wooded acres that had been my refuge as a child. As I drove out the long, tree-lined driveway of my childhood home for the final time, a simple image came to mind that gave me a way to talk about what I had been learning. It consisted of two parallel lines with a space between them.

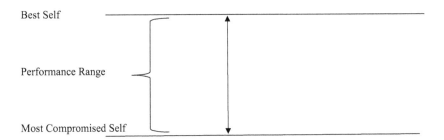

**FIGURE 2.1** The Range of the Self

The top line represents me at my best self, and the bottom line represents me at my worst. What helped me begin to thrive as a teacher was developing the capacity to hew as closely as I could to the top line and teach from there.

The version of me at the best-self line is the version who sat in that forest as a kid—open, relaxed, and curious. Walking into the chaotic house of my childhood, I would drop toward the bottom of that range. In my early years of teaching, day-to-day stressors and successes had me bouncing between the range's extremes. An out-of-control class would drop me to my most compromised self, while working with a particularly receptive student would lift me toward my best. I was like a dog on a chain being yanked by circumstances from one version of myself to another.

Human beings naturally get tugged around by circumstances because we are wired to react adversely to pressure. The greater the pressure, the more likely we are to fall toward the low end of our range, entering a place from which teaching becomes an unsustainable, miserable experience. The good news is that we don't need to get beaten up by martial artists to learn to be at our best under the pressure of teaching. For teachers, the classroom, with all of its challenges, can become a training dojo. By applying the principles presented in the chapters that follow, teachers can grow their capacity to respond to difficult circumstances from their best self. Moreover, when they teach from that state, their students will naturally respond from their best selves. This maximizes the chances for constructive learning while automatically making one of the toughest jobs on the planet considerably easier.

From our best self, we simply become better teachers. We gain influence with our students that we wouldn't otherwise have— influence that we can leverage to help them grow. The benefits of teaching from our best self are many and include the following:

1. Greater possibility of long-term positive impact on students.

Teachers want to help their students gain the skills and knowledge required for passing their class, but most teachers want to do more. We want to inspire students to keep learning long after their last day in our classroom. We want to teach them to persevere and not give up on themselves. The chance of having such a life-changing impact dramatically increases when we teach from our best self.

This was made poignantly clear to me a few years ago when, quite out of the blue, I received a notice that I was a finalist for a teaching award. When I read the name of the person who nominated me, I just about wept. It was a former student whose family had been decimated by the effects of poverty, drugs, violence, and alcohol. While in my class, his attendance was spotty; sometimes he would be absent for weeks at a time. Whenever he did show up, I would let him know I was genuinely glad to see him, often calling him up to my desk to talk about his attendance and the assignments he was missing, but also to ask how things were going, encourage him, and do my best to offer support. It would have been easy to become impatient and irritated with this young man. He was the kind of student teachers complain about in the staff room—students who make it impossible for teachers to feel successful. But I continued bringing him my best. It was months before he would actually converse with me. It was almost a year before he completed an assignment, a powerfully written narrative describing what he had been through in his life. A few months after that, he stopped coming to school and then dropped out entirely. I tried calling his home, but the phone number was disconnected. I often wondered what had happened to him.

In his nomination statement he wrote:

> Despite how many times I've broken my word or promises to complete projects and assignments, Mr. Schroder refused to leave me behind. He met with me more times than I can count. … No matter how many reasons I have given him to give up on me, he's given me twice as many not to give up on myself.

I later learned that this young man had decided to pursue his GED. I hope he's achieved that.

It's important to remember the power we teachers have when we bring our best—the positive influence we can bring to bear on a young life, even when it seems we are failing.

2. A chance to help close the achievement gap.

The achievement gap, whether it refers to the academic performance gap between racial groups or between children from lower and higher socioeconomic backgrounds, is one of the thorniest problems education faces. How can teaching from our best self help close this gap?

Research shows that the brains of children who grow up in a disadvantaged environment—whether due to racism, family stress, an unsafe neighborhood, poverty, or any other difficult context—become hypersensitized to the negative impacts of stress. They come to school with reduced neural connectivity in their prefrontal cortex, the part of the brain that allows for planning, problem solving, and regulating emotions—all critical capacities for academic success (Blair, 2012). So much in school (and in life) depends on a person's ability to persist through a difficult process toward long-term fulfillment, but the brain patterning of students with chronic stress in their backgrounds frequently inhibits them from easily doing this. Students who've experienced high stress loads have developed stronger stress response systems and weaker prefrontal cortexes, leaving them prone to making impulsive choices rather than the strategic, though uncomfortable, choices that could yield benefits later (Sapolsky, 2021).

When teachers feel pressured to get these students to learn and are frustrated in the attempt, they are prone to fall from their best self, potentially undermining the learning environment. This in fact worsens the problem, as research shows that a chaotic, poorly run learning environment impedes learning, particularly for disadvantaged youth. Conversely, reducing classroom stress for both teachers and students interrupts this negative feedback loop (Blair, 2012). When we teach from our best self, we retain the presence of mind to wind down the stress in the classroom. This gives students' overwrought brains a reprieve and, since young people's brains are exceptionally malleable, a chance to begin rewiring for success.

3.   Reduction in classroom management issues.

When teachers teach from their best self, students are less apt to act out. On the flip side, when teachers are tired or beset with stressors and they fall from their best, classroom behavior issues tend to magnify and multiply.

Brain science explains why. By hooking a monkey's brain to sensors, scientists could track how different tasks activated different parts of a monkey's brain. It wasn't until the 1990s, however, that they discovered that the same parts of the monkey's brain were activated not only when the monkey was performing an action, but also when the monkey saw another monkey performing the same action. Scientists named these brain cells that activate both when performing an action and when seeing that action performed by others "mirror neurons" (Garcia Cerdán, 2017). When we watch another person perform a complex task, our mirror neurons fire, setting up the brain patterning we need to learn that skill ourselves. Mirror neurons also explain why we smile when we see someone else smile, and why laughter and yawning are so contagious.

It is because of mirror neurons that the self from which a teacher teaches has such a large influence on students' openness and responsiveness to a lesson. When teachers teach from their best self, students are cued to respond from their best selves, dropping resistance and maximizing the probability of being receptive to whatever the teacher asks of them.

4.   Better quality of life for the teacher.

Imagine, after a typical day of teaching, walking out of your classroom feeling inspired. You have energy to go to the gym, go grocery shopping, make dinner. After that, you still have energy to read a book or write a blog, work on an art project, or practice guitar. If you're a parent, you play with your kids. If you're married, you flirt with your spouse and make dinner together. You have space to breathe. When your union rep asks if you can serve in some capacity, rather than thinking, "I'm so exhausted," you have the inner freedom to ask yourself, "Does this opportunity align with my values? Does it inspire me?"

Teaching from your best self allows you to approach the ninja ideal of *in shin tonkei*, achieving maximum results through minimal effort. This frees up your time and energy for the things you love.

5. Teaching becomes fun.

When you teach from your best self, the doors swing open to *zanshin*, that flow state in which your awareness shifts to a scale that can hold all the intricacies of the job, where teaching becomes a kind of sublime dance, an utterly absorbing experience that cannot easily be described because it transcends conventional language. Even words like "joy," "wonder," and "bliss" fall flat compared with what it's actually like. The ego and its fears, self-consciousness, doubts, and concerns simply dissolve in the flow of being and doing.

Some would consider such states mystical and out of reach for average people. However, I can testify that such states are real and attainable for every one of us. Though I'm not suggesting that you will enter into a numinous experience with every lesson you teach, as you learn to teach from your best self, you will increasingly find that you have a genuinely good time at your job, and, within those good times, some moments will rise toward peak experience that will leave you speechless and overcome by the beauty of what you have done.

All of this is possible, but only if we can develop the capacity to sustain our best self in the face of the challenge of teaching. The first step toward building this capacity is taking a good look at what it is about teaching that makes staying in our best self so difficult. A major factor has to do with our own brains and the elegant system that has helped human beings survive for hundreds of thousands of years.

**REFLECTION QUESTIONS**

*Grab a notebook and something to write with and respond to the following questions:*

1 What might be your version of my childhood forest—a place that fills you up, relaxes you, and helps you connect with what matters?
2 Describe a time when you were far from your best self. What was the circumstance, and how did it feel to be in that state?
3 Describe a time when you were in your best self. What was the circumstance, and how did it feel to be in that state?

# 3

# Mapping the Brain

## Teaching and the Stress Response System

Stress makes it hard to stay in our best self, but what makes this so? How does stress transform a compassionate, dedicated teacher into an impatient and grouchy proxy? To answer these questions, we need to understand what happens in our brains under stress.

The human brain is actually three brains in one: an outer brain wrapped around a smaller brain, and an even smaller brain nestled inside of that. The outermost layer, the neocortex, is the most recent addition from an evolutionary perspective. The neocortex gives human beings their capacity for higher-order thinking, analysis, reasoning, language, learning, memory, and creativity. Accounting for 76% of the human brain's volume, the neocortex is humanity's great advantage. It more than compensates for the fact that pound for pound, humans are weaker than other animals; have extremely long childhoods, which means we need a decade and a half of protection to avoid getting snacked on; and lack claws and fangs with which to defend ourselves. In spite of these disadvantages, our neocortex and its practically infinite learning capacity has enabled us to dominate the planet.

DOI: 10.4324/9781003360513-5

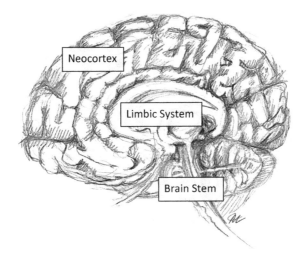

**FIGURE 3.1**  Diagram of the Brain

(Judy Lowe-Schroder)

Nested inside the neocortex is the limbic system, or midbrain, a group of interdependent cortical structures that include the thalamus, hypothalamus, hippocampus, and amygdala. Also called the mammalian brain, it is the brain's second evolutionary development. This part of our brain supports emotions and habitual behavior, evaluating everything we encounter as potentially pleasurable or painful and driving us to seek pleasure and avoid pain. It's the limbic brain that responds when an advertiser entices us with a sexy image, or when we find ourselves rubbernecking at the scene of an accident. The limbic brain does not apply logic and has no concept of time, so predicting the consequences of our actions is foreign to this part of our brain; we need the neocortex to help out with that. When under the sway of this part of our brain, we tend to act impulsively based on how we feel.

One of the limbic brain's main functions is assessing for threats. Think of it like the security checkpoint at an airport, where the TSA agents check ID and bags, making sure all passengers are safe to board the plane. If the limbic system determines a situation is safe, it authorizes admittance of the experience to the neocortex, where it can be processed and learned from. If the limbic system senses a threat, it kicks the whole system out of learning mode and into survival mode, setting off an alarm that alerts the third brain, the brain stem (also called the reptilian brain), to take over.

When undisturbed, the reptilian brain is like the breathing machine a person in a coma is hooked up to. It reliably regulates all the body functions we don't have to think about—breathing, heart rate, body temperature, balance. This frees up the rest of the brain to perform higher-order functions.

As soon as the limbic system detects a threat, it alerts the reptilian brain by flooding the body with adrenaline and epinephrine. The body becomes primed to fight, flee, or freeze. Blood and calories are pulled from nonessential areas, such as the neocortex, and directed to the muscles that will do the work of surviving. When your life or another's life depends on how fast you run, how ferociously you fight, or how completely you freeze, you want to perform as efficiently as possible—no thought, just do. This is the stress response system, and it is wonderful if you are fleeing a tsunami or fighting off a grizzly. Accounts in the news show people in life-or-death situations performing superhuman feats from this state—fighting off a mountain lion with their bare hands or lifting an automobile off a trapped person.

Researchers have identified a fourth kind of stress reaction that they've labeled the fawn reaction, or "please and appease." A person who reacts to stress this way is driven to please the source of the threat as a survival strategy. The fawn reaction is maladaptive, which means it is a learned response rather than an instinctual one. Children who grow up in trauma-based codependent relationships with primary caregivers are often trained to repress their natural, biologically driven fight, flee, or freeze responses and replace them with fawning.

Our limbic system is on the lookout for not only physical threats but also threats to our social standing and sense of belonging. You walk into the school building and the principal, instead of greeting you, gives you a curt summons to his office. You receive an accusatory email from a parent about a lesson you taught. That student in the back, the one glowering and slumped in his chair, has just ignored your request to sit up straight and follow along. When you ask him to sit up a second time, he says,

"This class sucks." Suddenly, the limbic system hits the button alerting the reptilian brain to initiate neocortex override, plunging you into fight, flight, freeze, or fawn, and you fall fast and hard from your best self.

Our students' brains function exactly the same way. Imagine you are that student, the one slumped at the back of the room. You want to be left alone because you're trying to recover from an argument you had this morning with your mom (who'd been drinking all night, and you awoke to her screaming at you). But the teacher, for no apparent reason, is hassling you, telling you to sit up straight, and there is a tone in her voice and you feel like she's running you down in front of the class. Suddenly, you want to punch something.

Once the limbic system activates the stress response, some time has to pass—generally 20 to 60 minutes in a safe, soothing environment—before it sends out the all-clear message and reengages the neocortex. One of the challenges of teaching is that teachers don't get those 20 to 60 minutes in a soothing environment to unwind themselves from fight, flee, or freeze.

Although the scientific literature calls the shift to fight, flight, or freeze a stress *response* (because the brain is responding to a potential threat), it is helpful to think of it as a stress *reaction*, because while in this state, a person will *react* to the situation rather than respond.

In a stress-reactive state, the limbic system reallocates resources from the neocortex to the heart, lungs, and muscles so the person can efficiently begin running, fighting, or freezing. Under the stressful conditions of education, it's not uncommon for a teacher to spend much of a day to some degree under the influence of a stress reaction. But for teachers to be effective, they need complete access to their neocortex.

Meanwhile, because stress reactions tend to be contagious, our reactive state is setting off stress reactions in our students, who, in turn, are setting each other off. Though teaching and learning are supposed to be happening, when the whole class is in survival mode rather than learning mode, neither teacher nor students have access to their whole brain. In a situation like this, meaningful teaching and learning are simply not possible.

It's worth wondering why people sometimes react so strongly to minor stressors. Can't the limbic system tell the difference between a cave bear and, for instance, a malfunctioning copy machine? Nope. The limbic system is not good at parsing subtleties. As far as it's concerned, a threat is a threat, and as soon as it senses one, it hurtles us into a stress reaction.

Three factors make people more vulnerable to stress reactions. The first is being tired, run down, or not feeling well. These states increase a person's susceptibility to losing it. Unfortunately, feeling tired and run down is a normal state for teachers.

Second, the limbic system does not register time—for it, past, present, and future, are one and the same. (This is why simply worrying about a possible future can throw you into a stress reaction. If you do this at night, hello, insomnia.) Because the limbic system is constantly on the lookout for patterns that signify danger, when a person encounters a situation that reminds it of a previous traumatic event, not only is the fight-flight-freeze alarm activated, but the person is thrown into an emotional and sometimes physical reaction to that previous trauma (discussed in further detail in Chapter 4), leaving the person feeling justified in whatever overreaction they bring to the situation.

Third, stress builds in a person's system; it accumulates until it reaches a tipping point and the limbic system pulls the stress reaction alarm. If a copy machine malfunctioned on an otherwise stress-free morning, it would register as a bother but likely not topple a teacher into a full-blown stress reaction. The teacher would be able to adapt to the circumstances and, in a pinch, come up with a creative solution to teach the lesson without those copies—the neocortex coming to the rescue with a burst of creativity.

But imagine your principal is coming in to observe you tomorrow. You work late the night before preparing the lesson, except for the copies you plan to make as soon as you arrive at school the next morning.

The next morning, however, you have some trouble getting your own children off to school, so you show up a few minutes late. As you hurry into the building, you see the principal standing in the hallway giving you the side-eye for being late.

You enter your classroom and turn on your computer. An urgent email from the dean says that a parent of one of your students has concerns and is coming in for a meeting in a few minutes. Instead of making the copies, you attend the meeting. You make a plan to get those copies made during the midmorning break, right before you need them. At the meeting, because you have access to your neocortex, you are able to clearly state your position in a way the parent understands. Still, the meeting is stressful.

You return to your classroom and greet students as they enter. You have a wonderful small-group activity planned, but when you try to implement it, a student gets mad about having to work in groups. He says he doesn't like one of the students you've grouped him with and refuses to join. Now you have a defiant student to deal with, but you are also worried about the student he called out—her feelings are probably hurt. You tell him to do as you've asked. He storms out saying, "I hate this fucking class," slamming the door as he goes. By the end of the exchange, you're trembling. "Get to work," you tell the rest of the students. You return to your desk to write out the referral.

Rather than take the assignment seriously, the students start talking about unrelated topics and joking with each other, but now, you don't feel up to confronting them, so you hunker at your desk writing the referral until the bell rings.

At the bell, you rush off to make the copies. You need to get them made fast; you don't want to be late to your own class, especially when your administrator will be observing you. When the copy machine jams, your limbic system does the job it is designed to do—you feel like a bomb goes off in your body.

You have a problem. You need to figure out how to fix the copy machine or come up with a way of delivering the lesson that doesn't rely on the copies. You need access to your neocortex, but that's pretty much offline. Your limbic system has activated the alarm, leaving you with a spear of adrenaline through your heart, a dry mouth, flushed face, a sped-up heart rate, trembling hands, and a sick feeling in your gut.

You know you can't flee or freeze, and there is nothing to fight but the stupid copy machine. You resist the urge to kick it. Yet all that energy has to go somewhere. In your mind, you begin beating yourself up—*Why didn't I make these copies yesterday? How could I be so stupid?*—or you find an external target to take it out on—*The incompetent administration at this school can't even keep a copy machine in working order. How do they expect me to do my job without a functioning copy machine?* Meanwhile, the seconds are ticking. Within a few minutes, the bell will ring, signaling the start of the class, and your principal will sit down in the back of your classroom and begin taking notes on everything you say and do.

We've all been there—different scenarios, but similar thoughts and feelings. When the limbic system hits the alarm and we cannot do what we're biochemically programmed to do in that moment—fight, flee, or freeze—we repress those physical urges even as the emotional and physiological reactions course through our mind and body. We swallow our distress, try to pretend we are fine. But we are far from fine, far from our best self.

What we need is time to wind down—time to take a walk, to breathe, to collect ourself—but we have a class to teach. So we teach that class, but we are likely irritable, closed down, impatient, aggravated by small things, easily upset. How can we be otherwise? We are a bottle under pressure and can't keep how we feel from squirting out around the cork. Nowhere to run, nowhere to hide; we just want to explode.

 **REFLECTION QUESTIONS**

*Grab a notebook and something to write with and respond to the following questions:*

1   List your job stressors and code each one as big, medium, or small.
2   Think of a time when, as a teacher, you were plunged into a stress reaction. What was the situation? What did the stress reaction feel like? What did you do or say?

# 4

# The Role of ACEs and the
# Hurtspots They Leave Us With

Stress reactions are often accompanied by emotions, particularly fear or anger. But sometimes the emotional content of a reaction goes beyond that; it may feel devastatingly intense or involve other emotions, such as shame or paralyzing anxiety. Often, these reactions are not simply stress reactions; they are reactions tied to past trauma.

As a young man, I noticed that some events plunged me into gut-wrenching emotions far out of proportion to the situation. Once I became a teacher and experienced the pressure of needing to "be on" all the time, these intensely emotional episodes became particularly troublesome. I noticed that these emotional spells could be triggered by a relatively minor event—a mildly critical email, for instance, or a student saying my class was boring. Once the emotions were initiated, I would feel them physically, like a punch in the gut or a stab in the heart. The bodily sensations would be accompanied by an avalanche of negative thoughts about myself that would persist for hours and sometimes days.

These dips into distress dramatically affected my performance as a teacher. When caught in their undertow, I would doubt if I was really cut out for this job. I looked for signs that other teachers were experiencing something similar, but if they were, they didn't talk about it. I would sit in professional

DOI: 10.4324/9781003360513-6

development trainings hoping to hear mention of something resembling this rather large elephant squatting in the middle of my own teaching experience. But serious conversations about education were exclusively focused on externals—rubrics, standards, methods, learning targets. The inner life of a teacher and how it affected teacher performance were entirely ignored. Since no one else was talking about having experiences like mine, I figured it was just me. I felt ashamed, like there was something wrong with me, so I didn't talk about them either.

I now understand that most adults periodically experience these kinds of intense emotional reactions, and that there are good reasons for them.

In 1994, Kaiser Permanente and the Centers for Disease Control initiated a study by asking 17,421 patients to complete a questionnaire about prior traumatic experiences (Felitti, 2002). For the next 15 years, the patients were tracked through their medical records and asked to complete questionnaires about finances, education, and marital status. The key finding of this study, known as the ACEs (Adverse Childhood Experiences) Study, was that adults who had suffered more severe and more frequent adverse childhood experiences grew up with a greater number of health problems of greater severity than adults who had experienced less trauma. Researchers found that ACEs correlated strongly with a dramatic increase in heart disease, diabetes, obesity, and early death. Notably, ACEs also negatively influenced mental health, with statistically greater rates of depression, substance abuse, poor academic achievement, divorce, and unemployment. Not only were adults who had suffered a significant number of ACEs living shorter lives; they were also leading harder ones.

This study showed that unresolved childhood trauma lives on in people's minds and bodies, negatively impacting them far into adulthood. ACEs change a person's brain development by strengthening the areas involved in stress reactions at the expense of the neocortex (Lewis, 2019). This sets their limbic system on permanent hypervigilance, making them highly prone to stress reactions. In addition, because the limbic system is especially on watch for situations similar to previous experiences that involved threat, people carrying unresolved childhood trauma are particularly susceptible to stress reactions that remind them of a past traumatic event. For instance, for someone who suffered trauma from a male authority figure, that side-eye from the principal in the previous chapter's scenario may be enough to trigger a full-blown limbic alarm. Someone who doesn't carry that trauma may register the side eye-as simple information (*Okay, he wants me here on time*) without tumbling into fight, flee, or freeze.

When people who carry unresolved trauma become triggered by a past event that reminds them of a previous trauma, the subsequent stress reaction is accompanied by a flood of distressing and intense emotions and even physical sensations. Their conscious mind, unaware of the deeper process unfolding, naturally looks to the real-time situation as the source of emotional distress, so the person reacts to that situation at the scale of the emotional pain they are experiencing. What looks to be an extreme overreaction from an observer's perspective feels entirely justified to the person feeling the pain.

I call these pockets of unresolved trauma that people carry around "hurtspots." Hurtspots set off hurtspot reactions when current-time events contain some element that spurs a recollection of the original trauma in the psyche.

A hurtspot reaction can severely impair a person's ability to function, dropping them far from their best self. A teacher in the throes of a hurtspot reaction may go through the motions of teaching a class, but because she is filled with painful emotions and carrying a mangled view of reality, she is likely to act in ways she wouldn't if she were at her best.

Besides impairing our ability to teach, spending a lot of time in stress reactions and hurtspot reactions also makes us miserable. Quite naturally, we begin counting down the days to summer vacation and fantasizing about having an easier job (meaning, one that doesn't trigger so many stress and hurtspot reactions).

From inside a hurtspot reaction, we feel terrible and automatically blame the present-time circumstances or the person whose actions awakened these awful feelings in us. But doing that will only ensure that the unprocessed emotions continue cycling around the blame. In time, the emotions will die down, and we'll put the episode behind us. The hurtspot will go into hibernation, certain to ambush us the next time we encounter a similar experience.

Many people live their whole life cycling in and out of reactions prompted by the same hurtspots, insisting on blaming others for their painful experiences. It's a trap.

To get out of it, we first need to stop blaming ourselves for being prone to tumbling into these dark holes of pain; for anyone carrying hurtspots, recurrent vexing episodes come with the territory.

Second, we need to stop blaming current-time circumstances for our hurtspot reactions and instead begin to identify patterns in the circumstances that prompt them. Recognizing which kinds of events stir up hurtspot reactions in us helps us realize that the current event did not cause these painful emotions; it merely dredged them up. This realization gives us the moment's pause we need to keep ourselves from acting out on those emotions.

Bringing hurtspots into the broader conversation in education allows us to recognize them as a factor that makes it extremely challenging for teachers to remain in their best self. In Part IV of this book, we will explore approaches that help to heal hurtspots. For now, it's worth saying that accepting the pain that a hurtspot stirs up and breathing into that pain can be useful. Just noticing and being aware of our inner experience allows our system to begin processing the unresolved emotional content associated with the original trauma, which is a step on the way toward getting our system to release the hurtspot and creating a more resilient best self.

 **REFLECTION QUESTIONS**

*Grab a notebook and something to write with and respond to the following questions:*

1   Begin compiling a list of the hurtspots in yourself that you are aware of, and note down the kinds of events, situations, or exchanges that trigger them.
2   Think of a time when a hurtspot in you was activated. Describe the situation. What was it like? What thoughts and judgments came up? What feelings and emotions arose?

# 5

# Stress, Pressure, and Hurtspots in Students

Like teachers, students experience stress in school, and high stress is toxic to learning. Although a low to moderate level of stress can heighten alertness and improve performance, when stress hits a certain threshold, it cripples executive functions in the brain that are critical for academic success (Blair, 2012). High stress can lead students to tip into stress reactions and worst-self behavior, further complicating the teacher's job.

The capacity for dealing with stress before succumbing to a stress reaction varies from student to student. Students who grow up in a high-stress environment are likely to grow up with hair-trigger limbic systems. For them, even mild school stressors can prompt their limbic system to initiate neocortex override. New research confirms that the brains of youth who have been exposed to high levels of stress develop patterns that make it harder for them to learn in school, contributing to achievement disparities between them and fellow students who grow up in less stressful environments (Heissel et al., 2017).

Some of the stressors students face in school are small things that aggregate, like sitting on a hard plastic chair all day beneath the subtle yet constant flickering of the banks of fluorescent lights. Other stressors are big, such as social pressures and fear

DOI: 10.4324/9781003360513-7

of feeling judged. For young people to feel at ease, they need to know they belong. Until they do, their limbic system constantly surveys the situation, calculating whether they are liked and how well they fit in.

While this background of anxiousness buzzes through the classroom, the teacher is teaching. This too may be stressful for students. What if the teacher calls on them and they don't know the answer? Will the teacher ridicule them? Will their classmates laugh? The threat of failure, of feeling humiliated, is real.

Even under the best of conditions, learning is stressful. Consider anything you've learned—perhaps how to drive, or how to play a song on the piano, or how to use an equation to solve a math problem. In every case, you went through a three-stage learning process: excitement about learning something new, stress and frustration in the process of learning it, and pride once you succeeded.

| Stage | Emotion | Thought | Description |
|---|---|---|---|
| 1 | Excitement (or at least a positive sense of possibility) | Cool, I want to do this. | You haven't acquired the knowledge or learned the skill, but you see the promise in the learning. You have a vision of yourself having learned, and you feel inspired to become that person. |
| 2 | Frustration, discouragement, stress | Ugh … this is hard. I don't think I can do this. Why am I even trying? | Once in the process of learning, you realize it is harder than you expected. You struggle, you make mistakes, you fail. As the difficulty of learning this information or skill becomes more clear, you may lose touch with the inspiration of stage 1. You may feel self-doubt. You may want to quit. |
| 3 | Pride | Wow, I did it! | You have succeeded, and you feel proud of your accomplishment. This builds your confidence so that the next time you set out to learn something new, you know you can persevere when it becomes difficult and succeed. Through multiple successful learning experiences, you build your confidence in your ability to learn new things. |

Some amount of stress is innate to stage 2 of the learning process. The doubt about whether we will be able to successfully learn and the frustration that wells up as we try is the felt experience as our brain builds the neural pathways required to do the task we are striving to learn. When learning gets derailed, it usually does so at stage 2.

For a learner whose brain is already burdened by stress, the frustration of the second stage may be so severe that it triggers a stress reaction, knocking him out of his learning brain into his survival brain. Such a student will likely give up before he reaches stage 3. If this happens often enough, he loses confidence in himself as a learner; he becomes reluctant to risk future failure when learning something new. Then the process starts going astray at stage 1, because instead of seeing possibility and feeling inspired, he feels anxious about failing before he even starts. A student in this condition will not even want to try. To a teacher, he appears shut down, resistant. Instead of engaging in the lesson, he may disrupt the class.

Complicating matters is the fact that most students don't experience the excitement of stage 1 in the classroom. This is because the academic subjects teachers are assigned to teach are not typically what students want to learn. To take advantage of the inherent benefits of stage 1, teachers must get students inspired about the material prior to teaching it, but teachers are not trained to do this or even told it's a good idea to try. Instead, teachers are trained to introduce the learning targets and then immediately launch into the lesson, thrusting students into stage 2 without the inspiring vision of stage 1. To compensate, teachers often try to motivate students with the threat of a failing grade, which only adds to the stress and pressure students already feel.

Imagine that you have succeeded at getting an entire class through stage 1, inspiring them about the learning to follow. So far, so good. Then the class moves into stage 2 and some students start demonstrating early signs of stress reactions. A few are complaining (a fight response). Others are sneaking glances at their phones or talking to their neighbors (both forms of fleeing), while a few try to become invisible so you won't call on them (freezing). You've been told that your success depends on your students' engagement, and your administrator expects to be able to walk into your classroom and see all students studiously engaged. The pressure of trying to get the students who are tipping toward fight, flee, or freeze to productively engage could easily trip you into a stress reaction, or even a hurtspot reaction. Caught in your own reactivity, maybe you raise your voice or threaten them with failure, but this only pushes them farther out of their learning brain and deeper into their reptilian brain, making a bad situation worse.

To help students successfully move through all 3 stages of the learning process, we need to minimize student stress by teaching from our best self. A student can endure quite a bit of learning-stress without falling into a stress reaction as long as the calm, reassuring presence of a teacher he trusts is nearby, someone who believes in him and is making learning safe.

Dealing with a single student having a stress reaction might be manageable, but it's more common that multiple students will flip into stress reactions almost simultaneously. This is because stress reactions are contagious. While on a walk in the woods, you may have encountered a small herd of deer standing placidly together; suddenly one deer gets spooked and bolts— immediately, the others join. Human beings are also wired that way. Our limbic system is designed to notice when people nearby are sensing a possible threat. Not wanting to take chances, if someone in our surroundings is reactive, our limbic system also flips the switch. This kind of contagion is reinforced and amplified by mirror neurons—the neurons that reflexively fire in mimicry of another person's actions or emotional state. One person gets antsy, and the next thing you know, everyone is panic-buying toilet paper.

Dealing with stress reactions in students is hard enough, but students can also experience hurtspot reactions in our class. Even seemingly minor things—another student bumping into them as they enter a room, an assignment that seems too hard or too long, a teacher asking them to put their phone away—can trigger a student into a hurtspot meltdown. As with a stress reaction, when this happens, it tends to activate other students, leading to a very rough day for a teacher.

Furthermore, teachers can create the conditions that engender new hurtspots in students. Frustrated teachers may do and say things that leave students feeling harshly criticized, or dumb in front of their peers. Even an off-hand comment can leave a mark, planting the seed for a hurtspot that negatively affects a young person's relationship to learning and to school.

In the moment when a teacher says or does the thing that produces a hurtspot in a student, that teacher is probably not in his best self. Likely, he is caught in the whirlpool of one of his own hurtspots. Activated hurtspots lead adults to speak and act in ways that create hurtspots in kids, who grow up to create hurtspots in the children in their lives. When we teach from our best self, we interrupt this awful passing of hurtspots down the generational line. Anyone who carries a hurtspot knows how it can squeeze down a person's life. The last thing we want to do is inflict this kind of long-term distress upon a young person in our care.

Attempting to teach students who bring keyed-up limbic systems and an assortment of easily activated hurtspots into the classroom can leave a teacher confused, hurt, and even desperate to flee the profession. However, understanding how stress and trauma affect both ourselves and our students can help us reorient around what matters. We can take care of ourselves while helping our students successfully navigate the challenges built in to learning.

Part II of this book explores approaches that will help teachers retain their best self under classroom pressure while increasing student receptivity and reducing the chances of hurtspots getting triggered. But first, there is one more massive force to consider, operating behind the scenes in the classroom, invisibly affecting everyone's ability to be in their best self: the force of culture.

**REFLECTION QUESTIONS**

*Grab a notebook and something to write with and respond to the following questions:*

1 Think of a time when you successfully learned a difficult thing. In terms of the three-stage learning process, how did you manage to keep from giving up in stage 2?
2 Recall a time when a student had a stress or hurtspot reaction in your classroom. What happened? What was that like for you as a teacher?

# 6

# Reckoning with the Impact of Culture

At the surface level, culture is often thought of in terms of music, ethnic food, costumes, and holidays shared and celebrated by members of a society. This is true as far as it goes. However, at a deeper level, culture is the stories, values, beliefs, symbols, and behavior norms that the members of that society collectively hold and identify with. Culture tells us what to believe, how to think, how to live. We participate in the creation of culture, while culture participates in the creation of us.

Culture wires the developing worldview of a child, seeding it with beliefs, biases, meanings, and definitions of success. By adulthood, these seeds have grown into a fully developed belief system that touches every facet of the person's life, influencing her point of view, what she pays attention to, how she defines status, and how she makes sense of her experiences. Although culture affects us all, it is so interwoven with our sense of ourselves that it is difficult to see. When culture speaks, it speaks with the voice in our head, providing ready-made ways of thinking and being that we presume originate from us. Culture gets so under our skin that we live mostly unaware of the effects of culture and the fact that we can actually question what culture tells us.

DOI: 10.4324/9781003360513-8

Subcultures, like the larger culture within which they are situated, have their own set of stories, biases, values, and assumptions. Examples of subcultures include the culture of an ethnic group, but also the culture of a corporation and the culture of a school.

The culture of a school is typically driven by the cultural values of the larger community of which the school is a part. For instance, in some community subcultures, attending college is expected. Students who live in these communities tend to regularly attend school and work hard, seeing the primary grades as preparation for high school and high school as a launching pad for college. However, in community subcultures in which academic achievement takes a back seat to other values, students are less likely to prioritize education. For good or ill, students bring their culture to school with them, sometimes relating to teachers as antagonists to the general cultural flow they most identify with.

Even high-achieving school cultures can be problematic, especially when status symbols of success are prioritized over deeper values of learning and education. I have always taught in communities where the prevailing subculture has a middling or even low estimation of education. My daughter, however, went to school in a town with a higher socioeconomic level than the surrounding communities and a correspondingly higher expectation of academic achievement. In that district, students who might otherwise have tended toward low achievement were swept up by the cultural current of the school and did what it took to fit in, even when that entailed several hours of homework every night.

In many regards, this was awesome. From kindergarten through her senior year of high school, I never once had to remind my daughter to do her homework. Yet I was concerned that she was taking her pursuit of grades to the extreme. She would spend hours on homework every night. She would go into tests so anxious that she would tilt into a stress reaction, losing partial access to her neocortex and scoring much lower than her actual ability should have reflected. Her grades suffered as a result, and this snowballed her into even greater anxiety for the next test.

Of course, I was proud of her and her work ethic, but I was also concerned that she was missing the big picture of what education is for, which in my mind is learning, not grades. For my daughter, cracking the code of what would earn an A from each of her teachers was the point. As she sat hunched at her desk doing homework in her room, I would sometimes pop in and ask what she was learning. She would look at me like I was speaking Martian. What did learning matter when grades were at stake?

What she did know was, to the hundredth decimal point, the GPA of each of her friends. The cool kids had high GPAs, and if you wanted to fit in, you did your homework and worked for A's.

I was particularly worried about how this obsession with grades affected her mental health. I wondered if the dark threat of a bad grade perpetually hanging over her head might ease if she intentionally failed a test; maybe she would see that the world doesn't end and she would be okay. It might help her relax. Playfully, I suggested she bomb a test on purpose, just for fun, to see what it was like. She adamantly refused. Instead, she would study through the night and then, at school the next day, let her stress reaction bomb it for her.

At my daughter's graduation ceremony of about 300 students, I sat on the grass in the town's park watching as all nine 4.0 valedictorians were introduced to uproarious applause. Grade point average was the currency of status at this school. My daughter still couldn't tell me what she had learned, but I already knew. She had learned to tie her self-esteem to grades, and to feel anxious about whether she was good enough as a result.

I tell this story to show the massive influence culture has on how students relate to school. Culture gets into us deeply. Every culture has positives and negatives, and there are things educators can do to amplify the positives and mitigate the negatives in a school's culture. Although difficult, it is also possible for a school to leverage the power of culture to intentionally create a shared set of school values and a shared narrative in which traits such as persistence, learning from setbacks, and doing one's best are celebrated. However, this entails every teacher, administrator, and support staff member consistently use the same language and take the same actions to affirm the chosen values and narrative. School policies need to be rewritten so they feed and support the created culture. Discipline policies need to defend the fledgling culture, even if this means giving students who refuse to buy into the new norms a different placement until they mature enough to participate in the school's culture productively. I am fortunate to have participated in the successful creation of one such school culture and witness how it transformed students' relationship to school and learning. The transformation lasted for a single year before our hard work was undone by the pandemic.

Attempting to shift an entire school's culture is a major whole-staff project. Short of that, individual educators can still turn their classrooms into protected bubbles of subculture in which learning, respect, and doing one's best are insisted on and celebrated. The principles in Part II of this book will help you turn your classroom into one of these bubbles of subculture that tends to bring out the best in students.

Just as culture influences the way students show up for school, the culture of the education system itself influences teachers. The voice of this culture speaks inside teachers' heads, providing ready-made assumptions about what it means to be a good teacher, saying things like:

*Good teachers sacrifice themselves for their students.*

*Good teachers put in extra hours late into the evening and on the weekends.*

*Because supply budgets are tight, for the sake of the students, good teachers reach into their own pockets to purchase classroom supplies or spend their summers crowd-funding for glue sticks and pencils.*

Axioms like these, ingrained in the culture of education, generally go unquestioned. But teachers who want to thrive in their job will need to question them and, from time to time, take contrary action to preserve their well-being.

Now that we better understand the challenges of teaching, we can explore practical approaches for sustainably leaning into that daunting mass of challenges from our best self.

**REFLECTION QUESTIONS**

*Grab a notebook and something to write with and respond to the following questions*:

1 How would you describe the culture in your school and district?
2 From your experience, what are some of the beliefs, assumptions, and norms that teachers hold about what it means to "be a good teacher"?

# Part II

## Skills and Principles That Matter

# 7

# Return on Investment

It was a beautiful October Sunday during my first year as a teacher—a perfect day for a bicycle ride, a walk in the woods, or a good book and a bench at the park. After breakfast, I stepped outside for a few gorgeous minutes. The air was cool, the sun warm, and the red-and-gold leaves on the maple in the front yard shimmered in the breeze. I inhaled it all, then went back inside. I sat at the kitchen table with a mug of coffee, took a big stack of essays from my messenger bag, and began grading. Grading essays seemed pivotal to being a good English teacher and I wanted to do it well. I recalled the comments my college professors would leave in the margins of my essays—encouraging comments perfectly calibrated to help me grow as a thinker and a writer. Now I was the one writing the comments, and I felt the weight of that. I read slowly and carefully, endeavoring to leave helpful, encouraging messages in the margins of my students' essays. I worked with pencil so I could erase and rephrase until I was satisfied. I graded and made comments all day and into the evening.

On Monday morning, I handed back the essays and then watched my students, waiting for them to read my notes, anticipating the lights going on behind their eyes, the quiet indications of "I see" and "aha." Instead, they glanced at the grades, briefly flipped through the pages, jammed the essays into their backpacks, and looked up at me as if to say, "Okay, that's done, now what?"

DOI: 10.4324/9781003360513-10

I was stunned. I had given up my Sunday. I had agonized over those comments. Most didn't even read them.

What I had done had a high cost for me but yielded a low benefit for them—a terrible return on my time, energy, and attention. I needed a better approach to grading, one that was less costly for me and more beneficial for students. But if I was going to thrive at this job, I couldn't stop there. I needed to redesign everything I did so it aligned with the true north of what actually mattered.

As we saw in the Introduction, the ninja warriors of ancient Japan called the pursuit of maximum impact with minimum effort *in shin tonkei*. A related idea in economics is return on investment (ROI), which is defined as the ratio of an investment's gain or loss relative to its cost. Just as investors want to invest the least amount of money for the maximum gain, teachers want their investments of time, energy, and attention to maximally benefit students. A teacher's time, energy, and attention are finite and precious; we want a big bang for every buck.

All too often, teachers exhaust themselves by doing things that don't matter, that don't deliver a positive ROI, leaving them with little energy for the things that do. Examining our job through the lens of ROI helps us notice where we might be pouring time, energy, and attention into things that both drain us and yield negligible student learning. Once we identify what isn't paying off, we can begin experimenting with an eye toward lower-effort/higher-impact teaching.

Whenever I introduce the concept of ROI to teachers, someone invariably asks what they should do about tasks and duties their administrators direct them to do that yield a low ROI. To that question, I have two answers. The first is that resisting assigned duties yields a terrible ROI; it saps our energy by producing the same kind of internal tension that I experienced in the dojo when resisting an opponent's attack. It also costs time—think of the escalating conversations with administrators about why we aren't fulfilling our professional duties. The stress is significant and nets nothing when it comes to student learning. Also, resisting directives expends our attention on things we can't change, breeding cynicism and quashing our passion for teaching.

My second answer is that if it's a task upon which your job depends, doing the task actually yields a high ROI *for you* so long as you value your job. Defying administrative directives puts your job in jeopardy. The benefit to you and the benefits you will be able to bring to your students as a result of keeping your job and maintaining a positive working relationship with your administrators should be part of any ROI calculation.

The skills and principles offered in the chapters that follow are the result of over two decades of looking at teaching through the lens of ROI. Each approach is designed to minimize our expenditure of time, energy, and attention by investing it in ways that help students the most. By strategically allocating these precious resources, we strengthen our capacity to maintain our best self under the pressures of the job. This creates a positive feedback loop, because when we teach from our best self, our students are more likely to respond to us from their best selves. When both teacher and students are bringing their best, we are well on our way toward *in shin tonkei*—low-effort, high-impact teaching.

---

 **REFLECTION QUESTIONS**

*Grab a notebook and something to write with and respond to the following question:*

1 List the tasks you perform. Rate each task high, medium, low, or none with regard to yielding positive ROI.
2 What, in your experience, really matters when it comes to teaching and learning? How do you know it matters?

# 8

# The Best Self Model for Teaching and Learning

Our current education system has its roots in nineteenth-century ways of thinking about how people learn. In the early 1800s, most schools were private schools where wealthy families sent their sons, and of those, the vast majority were religious schools. In the United States, these schools were particularly influenced by Puritan beliefs and the idea of original sin. Childhood was seen as a perilous period for a person's soul, and successfully navigating this period required the strong hand of a controlling authority to guide students through their lessons. So classroom learning was regimented, with the teacher insisting on structure and discipline and often resorting to corporal punishment to make sure students complied. The belief in an authoritarian-style school master as the source of knowledge followed the movement of education from private to common schools (what public education was called in the nineteenth century). Teachers were both the authority and the source of knowledge, standing at the front of the classroom and transmitting education, while students received the knowledge and recited it back. The belief was that student learning depended on what the teacher did.

During this same period, the Industrial Revolution was transforming the economy. As early public school advocates looked for models to efficiently educate large numbers of children, the production process of factories seemed a good model for schools:

DOI: 10.4324/9781003360513-11

students came to school as raw material that the teacher shaped and fashioned. Then students were passed from one grade to the next like products moving on an assembly line.

Although modern schools have, for the most part, abandoned recitation and corporal punishment, the idea that learning happens because of what teachers do is so pervasive that it's simply taken as unquestioned truth. Following the logic that the decisive ingredient to learning is what a teacher does, if students aren't adequately learning, then the teacher either isn't doing enough or isn't doing the right things in the right way to be effective. Hence, improving student performance requires giving teachers new and additional things to do, and then developing policies of oversight and accountability through which administrators can ensure that teachers are doing everything they are supposed to be doing.

As the outcome of this line of thinking, teachers face a continuous and ever-expanding crush of new mandates while working under increasingly restrictive policies that essentially rob them of professional agency. This leaves teachers stressed out and harried—caught in versions of themselves that are much less effective than their best for doing a job as complex as teaching.

Akin to the idea that student learning is dependent on what the teacher does is the assumption that the best way to make sure people do what we want them to do is through pressuring them. This reliance on pressure to get people to do what others want was built in to nineteenth-century society in a variety of ways. The model parent was a strict authoritarian. Industrialists pressured factory workers with threats of being fired. In schools, students were punished for not being able to recite the lesson. A century and a half later, the hammer of pressure is still ingrained into every level of education.

In school districts, pressure starts at the top and flows down. School boards want test scores to increase, so they pressure superintendents who pressure administrators who pressure teachers to do more.

The pressure on teachers comes from other directions as well. Lack of time is a big source of pressure, as there is simply not enough time inside the contractual hours for teachers to fulfill all the mandates and follow all the policies while also designing and implementing lessons, grading student work, participating in meetings, and performing other required duties.

Also, teachers put pressure on themselves. Teachers want to do well, so when they are struggling to keep up with all the demands, they are susceptible to pressuring themselves to work harder, to work later, to do more.

For students, pressure, especially pressure from the threat of failure, is built into the education system. Teachers heighten this pressure when they threaten students with failure, punishments, or loss of privileges, or when they criticize them for not productively engaging in the lesson. The belief in pressure is so deep-seated that when it fails to compel compliance, rather than wondering if pressure is the best approach, the pressure is increased until the student resentfully gives in or drops out.

In this way, schools become pressure-based coercion machines in which pressured teachers pressure students. The net effect is that students dislike school; the joy is sapped out of learning, leaving students with drastically reduced chances of becoming life-long learners.

The Best Self Model for Teaching and Learning starts with two assumptions about what helps people learn that are very different from the inherited nineteenth-century ones. First, in contrast to the belief that learning is determined by what teachers do, experience suggests that the self the teacher brings to the classroom matters more than what the teacher does. This isn't to say that the methods and practices the teacher employs don't matter, because they do. However, the state of being of the teacher is a greater determining factor when it comes to student learning. When teachers make choices about instructional methods from their best self, those choices are likely good ones. When teachers execute those methods from their best self, the chances of those methods working are maximized.

The second presumption embedded in the Best Self Model of Teaching and Learning is that stress and pressure are generally counterproductive for both students and teachers. Teachers are already intrinsically motivated to do their best for their students, and putting additional pressure on teachers actually impairs their ability to be effective. Likewise for students, more than enough pressure is already built into schools and learning. Adding more pressure risks tipping them into stress reactions, impairing their ability to learn and inciting resistance.

Given these assumptions, the Best Self Model for Teaching and Learning asserts that what matters most—what yields the greatest ROI—boils down to three mutually interdependent factors:

1.  The teacher teaching from their best self.
2.  The teacher relating to students in ways that support the students to be in their best selves.
3.  The creation of a learning environment that brings out the best in both teacher and students, turning classes into mutually supportive learning communities.

Each element in the model synergistically reinforces and amplifies the other two. For instance, when the teacher is in her best self, her students are influenced to interact with her from their best selves, which in turn improves the learning environment. Likewise, when the teacher interacts with students in ways that bring out their best, she has an easier time remaining in her best self, which again improves the learning environment. Correspondingly, when the teacher takes intentional steps

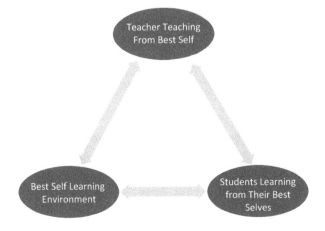

**FIGURE 8.1** Best Self Model for Teaching and Learning

toward creating and defending a learning environment based on safety, inclusivity, and belonging, this helps her students stay in their best selves, which makes it easier for her to stay in hers.

These three mutually reinforcing points (the self the teacher brings, the selves the students bring, and the quality of the learning environment) have always acted on one another. However, because education has been trapped in the old assumptions, these points have tended to interact in ways that increase teacher stress and harm student receptivity to learning. For instance, when the teacher slips from her best self into a stress or hurtspot reaction, she is likely to interact with her students in ways that drive them from their best selves, which then compromises the sense of safety in the learning environment. Likewise, if the learning environment is chaotic and haphazard, the students are less likely to retain their best selves, making it harder for the teacher to stay in hers. And when the students relate to the teacher from something less than their best, the teacher becomes more likely to tip from her best self, undermining the quality of the learning environment.

Although the education system as a whole still runs on the old assumptions, you don't have to. Each chapter that follows offers concrete approaches that address one of the three points of this model. The majority of the approaches support the teacher to maintain her best self, because the self she brings gives her the greatest leverage point the teacher has in the classroom.

---

 **REFLECTION QUESTIONS**

*Grab a notebook and something to write with and respond to the following questions:*

1  What is something you already do to take care of you, helping you bring your best to your job and to the people in your life?
2  What are some things you already do to support students to bring their best self to your classroom?
3  What are some things you already do to create a safe and inviting learning space that, in turn, helps create a community of learners?

# 9

# An Antidote to Decision Fatigue

## Finding Clarity through Reflective Writing

Teachers make a lot of decisions. The job requires thousands of split-second decisions that range in consequence from *Is this a good time to give Sheila permission to use the restroom?* to *Should I notify the police about these gun drawings in a student notebook?* Demands on teachers to make decisions come in an ongoing rush.

Early in my career, making so many decisions wore me down. As the day stretched into the afternoon, I would struggle to make the kinds of decisions that had been easy for me in the morning. By evening, I couldn't even decide what to have for dinner.

Every decision a teacher makes costs a bit of mental energy. By the end of the day, a teacher may have little mental energy left, leaving her with an inability to think clearly and a sense of feeling drained. Researchers call this decision fatigue.

The discovery of decision fatigue began with research on will-power. In the 1990s, social psychologist Roy Baumeister ran a series of experiments in which he taxed people's self-control and then gave them a demanding cognitive task to perform. In one study, he teased people with freshly baked treats, filling the room with

DOI: 10.4324/9781003360513-12

the sights and smells of chocolate chip cookies. A control group was allowed to eat the cookies, but the test subjects, after smelling and seeing the cookies, were made to eat radishes. After the food trickery, each participant was asked to complete a difficult puzzle. Those who ate the radishes gave up far sooner than the participants who indulged in the cookies. It was as if something had become tired in the radish-eaters' brains (Villarica, 2012).

Baumeister called this phenomenon "ego depletion." He hypothesized that people have a limited amount of mental energy, and that exerting willpower consumes this mental energy.

As other researchers took Baumeister's results further, they found that making decisions has the same deleterious effect on mental energy as exerting willpower. A 2011 study of 1,112 judicial rulings in Israel showed that prisoners who appeared before judges in the morning were paroled 70% of the time, while those who appeared late in the day were paroled less than 10% of the time (Danziger et al., 2011). The mental work of making so many consecutive decisions wore down the judges' ability to make decisions, until their decision-making ability was so depleted that, rather than struggling to make tough calls, they took the safe route of not paroling the prisoners.

But it isn't just weighty decisions, like deciding whether to parole a prisoner or put him back in prison, that lead to decision fatigue. In another study, researchers set out a series of desirable objects and told subjects they could take one home, but first they had to answer a series of questions. The questions were trivial, such as: Do you prefer a pen or a candle? An almond-scented candle or a vanilla-scented one? A candle or a T-shirt? A black T-shirt or a red T-shirt? While the research subjects were making decisions, a control group was simply told to contemplate the objects. Then all participants were tested on how long they could hold their hand in ice water. The subjects who had made trivial decisions lasted less than half as long as the control group who weren't asked all the questions (Tierney, 2011).

Because teaching is such a decision-demanding job, teachers are extremely prone to decision fatigue. In a decision-fatigued state, teachers are far from their best self. Common symptoms of decision fatigue are inability to think clearly, frequent procrastination, avoiding decision-making tasks, irritability, impulsiveness, feeling overwhelmed and hopeless, dissatisfaction with whatever choice is made, and spending an inordinately long time on individual decisions.

One approach to lessening decision fatigue is making policy decisions. A policy decision is one decision made ahead of time that guides future decisions, eliminating the cost in time, energy, and attention of making many individual decisions later. Famously, both Barack Obama and Steve Jobs made policy decisions about what they wore. In Jobs's case, that meant jeans and a black turtleneck every day. While president, Obama wore either a gray or a blue suit. Having to make even one less daily decision can help. Prioritizing ROI is a policy decision because it will guide a teacher's future decisions about what is most deserving of his limited time, energy, and attention.

## Decision Fatigue and Internal Conflict

One reason decisions are so expensive is that the decision-making process often stirs up internal conflict. Although people like to think of themselves as singular beings, each of us is more like a village containing a multiplicity of aspects, each aspect with its own voice, all wanting and needing different things, often at the same time. For instance, notice the arguments you have with yourself. Maybe one part of you wants to go to the gym and another part wants to sit on the sofa watching Netflix and eating Doritos. If you choose Netflix and Doritos, the internal conflict isn't necessarily over. The part of you that wanted you to go to the gym may continue piping up, berating you for being lazy, while you are trying to enjoy yourself. So maybe you eat more Doritos, have another glass of wine—anything to quiet that voice so you can enjoy the show in peace.

Internal conflicts arise from competing needs or loves. Because teachers are typically emotionally invested in the success of their students, they are vulnerable to frequent and expensive internal conflicts. You want to follow district mandates on curriculum, but you also want to teach things that are meaningful and that inspire your students. You want to eat your lunch in peace so you can gather yourself for the afternoon, but you also want to help the student who comes into your classroom wanting to talk. There is a department-wide policy on due dates, but a student shows up one day late with tears in her eyes and an assignment in her hand.

Experiencing these internal tugs of war is stressful. Having to make thousands of decisions each day from an internally conflicted place can be ruinous.

## Decisions versus Choices

Although the words "decision" and "choice" are often used interchangeably, they are distinct, as they involve different internal processes. For the purposes of this book, let's define decisions as making a selection based on a desire to achieve an outcome. In other words, we make decisions to get what we want or avoid something we don't want. When Baumeister coined the term "ego depletion," he was talking about depletion of that part of ourselves that consciously strategizes toward getting favorable results, typically results that move us away from pain and toward pleasure.

From this definition, decisions tend to activate internal conflict because different aspects within us want different things simultaneously, as we saw in the example of going to the gym versus watching Netflix. To successfully make a decision, we need to override the part of ourselves that wants something else. This consumes mental energy. A classroom teacher who has been making decisions all day may have used up her mental energy and at the end of the school day is unable to muster the necessary willpower to get herself to the gym. This, by the way, is one reason why simply telling teachers to practice self-care doesn't actually help them.

Also, decisions made from an internally conflicted state tend to be weak when it comes to resolve. If the teacher manages to make the decision to go to the gym, but just as she is headed out the door, her boyfriend suggests they order from DoorDash and watch a movie instead, he's essentially siding with the Netflix-and-Doritos side of her, aligning against the part of her that wanted to go to the gym. This could easily be enough for her to put her gym bag back in the closet and settle down on the sofa.

We can define choices, on the other hand, as selections we make that spring from our core values, our genuine nature. A person making a choice between working out and relaxing in front of the television would make their choice from their ground of being rather than calculating from a desire. She would ask: *Given the context of my life right now, what do I genuinely choose to do?*

Choices connect us with purpose. Because they come from our deeper, authentic nature, they tend to inspire our various internal aspects to align rather than quarrel, transforming our feuding village into an organization, with all the parts lined up behind the choice. We go to the gym undivided, lifting weights or running on the treadmill with a sense of clarity and purpose. This not only conserves our energy because we aren't fighting ourselves; a choice made from a place of internal alignment carries more weight than a decision. Choices connect us to our passion and energize us, helping us move through the day with a confident integrity, making us much less vulnerable to decision fatigue.

## Reflective Writing as a Doorway to Internally Aligned Choice

In order to arrive at choice, we have to make friends with our deeper nature, our core values, what we stand for—to follow that ancient Greek maxim, "Know Thyself." The kind of deep self-knowledge that allows a person to make internally aligned choices is actually rare—human beings don't typically come by it naturally—but we can grow our self-awareness and begin to become conscious of our own deep currents of purpose. One of the best ways to do that is through reflective writing.

Reflective writing allows us to reflect upon, process, and integrate information, events, and experiences through the lens of what really matters to us. Whenever I feel like my job is getting away from me—when I feel lost, overwhelmed, anxious, or uncertain—I pick up a pen and a notebook and write my way to clarity. Along the way, I discover things about myself that allow me to take future action with internal cohesion. Over the years, reflective writing has yielded a massive ROI, as it has allowed me to stay oriented toward the true north of what I value most and, in the context of my whole life, what matters most.

Reflective writing starts with a question. Research shows that the type of question is important. One of the most common introspective questions is "why." Why did I do that? Why do I feel this way? It turns out that "why" is one of the worst questions for building self-awareness. Asking "why" keeps us on the surface where opinion and judgment live, never allowing us to penetrate to the deeper layers of ourselves. In addition, "why" leads into ruminative patterns that can make us feel anxious or depressed (Eurich, 2018).

When it comes to building self-awareness, "what" questions are much better questions. For instance, after an upsetting exchange with a parent, rather than asking "Why did that bother me so much?" it is better to ask, "What other situations have left me feeling like that?" and "What can this experience show me about what I truly value?"

Bravely asking the big questions, such as "What do I really stand for?" and "What values are most important to me?" and then using writing to find our way toward self-awareness can awaken the clarity we need to make genuine choices that our internal villagers can align behind. Reflective writing can bring us closer to internal wholeness, a state in which our life is purposeful and our choices carry weight. Rather than being drained by decisions, we can be enlivened by choices organized around a meaningful purpose. This frees us to move through our day free of internal conflict, opening the door to teaching from a flow state, from *zanshin*.

**REFLECTION QUESTIONS**

*Grab a notebook and something to write with and respond to the following questions*:

1   What is one situation about which you experience internal con-flict in your job as an educator?
2   What are the various voices within you saying regarding that situation? What does each voice want?
3   At the deepest level you can access, what do you stand for as a person and as an educator? Use writing to extend your curios-ity, reaching for your deepest clarity, something that all of your internal villagers align behind.

# 10

# Spheres of Control and Influence

With the passing of the No Child Left Behind Act in 2001, education entered the age of data collection. That bill mandated that districts administer standardized tests to gauge school and teacher effectiveness. The test scores would be used to hold schools accountable to the public through school, district, and state "report cards" published every year. In theory, district leadership could use the data gleaned from the tests to inform policies and educational practices that would improve teaching and learning. But because the standardized tests used to create these report cards were not built to be diagnostic, this promise never panned out.

I was intrigued by the idea of using data to improve educational outcomes and started finding ways to track data in my classroom. I began by counting the number of students who passed my classes each term. I compared my students' standardized test results with the results of students in other teachers' classes. As a creative writing teacher, I compared the number of writing contest winners from my class with the number of winners from other teachers' classes across the state. Although I told myself I was constructively using data to improve, in fact my data collection had a dark side: I was keeping score to buttress my self-esteem and feel good about myself as a teacher.

My data-driven self-esteem ran into a crisis when I took a job in alternative education. At this school, the percentage of

DOI: 10.4324/9781003360513-13

students who earned credit in a given term was low due to inconsistent attendance. Some students had unstable home situations, and some were working full-time jobs. Mental health was a frequent factor in their choice to skip, as was stress at home. For them, attending school was less important than dealing with the difficult situations they faced outside the classroom. Their brains were in survival mode. School seemed like an additional stress, and, unlike the other stressors in their lives, they could temporarily eliminate school stress by simply not showing up.

Attendance was a schoolwide problem, so the principal directed each teacher to set an attendance goal for the students on their roster. Keeping score was right up my alley, and I jumped in, applying everything I could think of to raise attendance in my classes.

For years I had been told that the best way to increase attendance was to design engaging lessons, so I redoubled my efforts in this regard. I would frequently work late, writing brand-new, beautiful lessons that only a handful of students would show up for. I made hundreds of phone calls to students' homes and had long conversations with parents who were as exasperated by their son's or daughter's attendance as I was. I created worksheets for students to track their own attendance and calculate their own attendance percentages. I also had students set attendance and graduation goals for themselves and held conferences with them about their progress toward their goals.

I did all of this and more. Here's the punchline: although these were good things to do, my attendance numbers didn't budge. If student attendance was the measure of success, I was netting a terrible ROI. But I continued on, trying to discover the secret recipe that would cause all my students to attend.

One day, the bell for first period rang and no one showed up. Not a single student. Ashamed, I closed the door, not wanting other teachers to see my failure.

While sitting in my empty classroom, I began asking myself questions about agency. Was I a bad teacher because I was spending first period in an empty room? I sure felt like it. What could I have done differently, done better? I started wondering about what I actually had control over and what I didn't. In the critical moment when a student made the decision to skip or come to school—when their alarm rang in the morning, when a buddy during lunch said, "Hey, let's go to the river"—how much weight did my engaging lessons carry? Not much. This called to mind a graphic I had seen in Stephen Covey's *The Seven Habits of Highly Effective People* regarding control and influence.

The graphic consists of two concentric spheres. The central sphere contains all the things over which we have control. Control means that we can, 100% of the time, directly make something happen. Mostly what we can control is limited to ourselves: what we do and say, the choices we make. For instance, I have control over whether to pick up a stapler and place it in a drawer. I have control over whether to pour myself a second cup of tea. I have control over what I say to someone and what I put my attention on.

The outer concentric sphere contains everything over which I have influence. Influence means I have a say and my say gets factored in with all the other forces involved in bringing about a result. As I write this, an election is approaching, and each voter will have a tiny influence on the outcome. If I want to increase my influence on that outcome, I can move to a swing state, or I can donate time and money toward a particular campaign. But I cannot directly control who gets elected.

Unlike the binary nature of control—you either have it or you don't—the sphere of influence contains a range. In the graphic, things over which we have greater influence are plotted

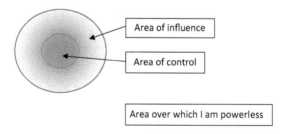

**FIGURE 10.1** Sphere of Control and Influence

Source: Adapted from Covey (1989); Aguilar (2018, p. 271).

closer to the sphere's inside edge, near the sphere of control. Things over which we have less influence are plotted closer to the outer edge of the sphere. The amount of influence most of us have over a national election would be a point plotted far toward the sphere of influence's outer edge, while the amount of influence a teacher has over the atmosphere in his classroom would be plotted closer to his sphere of control.

The space outside both spheres represents what we can neither control nor influence—the things we may worry about but have no way of affecting. Relatively speaking, what lies within our combined spheres of control and influence is a drop of water within the vast ocean of things over which we are powerless.

When it comes to wielding influence, the context, meaning the surrounding circumstances and overall situation, matters. For instance, a teacher will have more influence with a student if their interactions occur in the context of a trusting relationship. Likewise, a teacher will often have better results speaking to a student one on one rather than trying to have the same conversation in front of the class.

Timing matters, too. At different times a student will be more or less open to a teacher's influence. "Teachable moments" arise when, due to a convergence of factors outside the teacher's control, a particular lesson or concept is suddenly freighted with the power to be especially influential. Teachers can take advantage of moments like these to teach lessons when they are most likely to be impactful.

We exert influence through doing things that are within our control—through our state of being and what we do and say. A teacher can exercise control over the design of lessons and the choices she makes as she executes those lessons. Those choices then influence whether or not her students are engaged and learning.

The sphere of control and the sphere of influence might as well be different worlds, as each has its own rules and methods for achieving success. In Chapter 1, we saw that the only populations who are systematically forced to undergo a process they have not agreed to are prisoners, people getting arrested, and students. Prison guards and law enforcement officers are sanctioned, as well as given the training and equipment, to use force to control suspects and prisoners. Teachers, however, are relegated entirely to the realm of influence with regard to their students. A good teacher may appear to have control over a class, but actually she is wielding influence, and the students, out of trust and respect, are willingly going where she takes them.

Under pressure to get students to engage and learn, teachers may attempt to use control tactics such as shaming, scolding, threatening, criticizing, punishing, bribing, and yelling or snapping at students. These approaches are based in the old authoritarian style of teaching that says pressure is the best way to get students to do what the teacher wants them to do. One reason this doesn't work is that students are not actually in the teacher's sphere of control. Trying to control people who are outside of your sphere of control is a sure-fire way to burn yourself out.

Moreover, no strategy of control will ever inspire students to want to learn. Misguided attempts to control students simply exhaust teachers, removing them from their best self while driving students deeper into antipathy and disengagement.

Control-based approaches edge students closer to stress and hurtspot reactions while disabling a part of their brains, the seeking system, that when engaged, inspires them to want to learn. The seeking system is what motivates humans to explore, to learn, and to create meaning. When our seeking system is activated, we feel purposeful, vital, and most alive. Under conditions in which people feel controlled, their seeking system is swept aside, and their fear system takes its place. The fear system narrows their perceptions, making them anxious, dull, and depressed (Cable, 2019). With the fear system in charge, if students do comply, it's only because of their aversion to the pressure they have been threatened with, not because they are inspired to engage in meaningful learning.

A teacher's influence is the source of magic in the classroom. Influence is a relational power that involves an entirely different skillset from that of control. To effectively wield influence requires us to be in our best self. Influence requires building relationships based on trust. It requires being open, listening, accepting, and being curious about another human being's experience.

Knowing what belongs in each sphere really matters. We can needlessly drive ourselves to despair, as I did, by thinking we should be able to control things over which we have no control, or influence things over which we have no or only miniscule influence. In fact, trying (and failing) to control what cannot be controlled can induce helplessness and depression (Sapolsky, 2021).

It's easy to be swayed by the control-centered language that pervades education: *Control your class. Get these kids to graduate. If your students aren't attending, it's because your classes aren't engaging enough. All your students need to score at least a _____ on the state test.* That any of these are directly in our power is pure fiction. Believing and acting on these falsities is demoralizing and exhausting, and a likely route to teaching in ways that pressure students and disable their seeking systems.

That morning when I sat in my empty classroom dejected and embarrassed, I turned to reflective writing to reconsider the flawed foundation upon which I had built my self-esteem. In my notebook, I began having an honest conversation with myself about my limitations—what is and is not under my control.

I saw that the learning and behavior outcomes of my students were entirely beyond my control. I also saw that my self-esteem was too important to be built on a lie. I had to let go of the erroneous belief that I had any control over whether a student, on hearing his alarm go off in the morning, would decide to come to school and show up to my first period class. But I could make a promise that the students who did show up would get my best, every day. I could ground my self-esteem in that. That I could control.

Sorting out what exists in each sphere is a critical step on the journey toward achieving a greater ROI. When it comes to influence, the most important factor is you. Prioritizing what preserves and sustains you makes it easier for you to teach from your best self, which is the most important ingredient in positively influencing the growth and learning of the students in your care.

**REFLECTION QUESTIONS**

*Grab a notebook and something to write with and respond to the following questions:*

1   Draw a three-column chart. Head the columns as follows: Control, Influence, Powerlessness. Consider things that are pertinent to your job as an educator: under Control, list things over which you have control; under Influence, list the things over which you have influence but no control; and under Powerlessness, list the things that you'd like to have some power over even though you have neither control nor influence over them.

2   Looking at the Influence list, rank on a scale of 1 to 9 (with 1 being lowest and 9 being highest) how much influence you actually have for each item.

3   Applying the principle of ROI to control and influence: what are some things over which you have no control and very little influence that are consuming quite a bit of your time, energy, and attention?

# 11

# Applying Radical Acceptance to Teaching

It's easy as teachers to waste a lot of energy getting riled up about things over which we have no control—facilities and equipment in disrepair, technology breakdowns, inadequate supply budgets, unsupportive leadership, toxic school cultures, unreasonable expectations, disruptive student behavior, disrespect, too much to do … the list goes on. Not only is it exhausting to resist things over which we have no control and very little influence, it also reduces our chances of effecting positive change. We can better take care of ourselves and increase our likelihood of making a positive difference with a mindset of radical acceptance.

One Friday afternoon, an opportunity arose for me to teach my daughter about radical acceptance. Every Friday after work, when I picked her up at her mom's house for our weekend together, I'd ask her what she wanted to do. Quite often, she wanted to go to Yogurt Hut. One particularly sunny Friday, we decided to eat our yogurt on a bench out on the sidewalk. We were partway through our yogurts when a dark cloud suddenly rolled in above us and unleashed a torrent of rain. Because we were seated under an overhang, we could comfortably watch the storm. But the surprise downpour caught people without jackets, and there was not an umbrella in sight. The people scurried by us, doing what people do when caught in a cold rain:

DOI: 10.4324/9781003360513-14

hunching their shoulders, scrunching their faces. Then a young man walked by, upright and relaxed; he seemed unbothered by the rain. I asked my daughter if she thought he was getting any wetter than the people who were trying to hunch their bodies into tight balls. She said no; everyone was getting equally wet. Sometimes, I said, it's going to rain. The question is, are we going to resist it, or accept it?

This young man was radically accepting the rain. Rain, like many things in life, is outside our realm of control. Accepting, rather than resisting, whatever is actually so is one of the best ways to preserve our time, energy, and attention so we can use these precious resources to do something useful.

To understand what I mean by radical acceptance, it's useful to consider what it is not. Radical acceptance doesn't mean approval or endorsement. It doesn't mean I agree with it, or that I am resigned to it. Radical acceptance does, however, mean that I accept the fact of whatever is happening. Although I may speak out against it, do something about it, or take action to change it, I am not fighting the fact that reality is this right now. Radical acceptance is a life attitude in which a person receives rather than resists each moment, each situation.

I first learned about the power of radical acceptance as a very green second-year teacher facing a particularly unruly group of students. As an English teacher, I would share the literature which I most treasured, only to have my students complain about how boring it was. I would pose what I thought were relevant, thought-provoking discussion questions, and they would sit there sullenly or ignore me entirely while talking among themselves. I began feeling like the teacher in a *Peanuts* cartoon, a voice droning in the background, "wah wah who wah wah."

As I mentioned in Chapter 1, I came to teaching thinking my students would be attentive, curious, open, invested in wanting to grow and learn. The students in my classes, however, didn't match the students in my mind at all. These students didn't seem to care about literature or the discussion topics I posed. Faced with this incongruity, I began judging my real students for failing to measure up to my imaginary ones: *They should take their education more seriously. They should care about the topics I'm presenting. They shouldn't be disruptive.* I hardened around these judgments, especially around the word "should."

Since I had yet to learn that I have only influence, not control, over my students, I used the tactics one uses when attempting to control disruptive students: shaming, blaming, punishing—trying to force them to be what I thought they should be. Of course, none of that inspired my students to do anything but resist me and my attempts to teach them. Naturally, they hated my class. I had created an environment that was judgmental and unwelcoming.

I justified my approach by telling myself that I was holding high standards. But in fact, I was trapped in an attitude of resistance, draining myself by fighting against reality and heading down a dark path toward cynicism and bitterness. What I had yet to realize is that reality is bigger than we are, and trying to fight it will break us.

One November afternoon, after a particularly trying morning, I had an epiphany. I was standing in front of my third-period class looking into their faces when I recognized that I was holding so hard onto my idea of how my students should be that I'd disconnected from the students right in front of me. I would never be able to effectively teach these students, the ones sitting in the desks in my classroom, if I didn't first accept them as they were. In fact, accepting them as they were in that moment was an absolute prerequisite to having any influence at all that might help them grow into better students.

After this epiphany, my experience of teaching changed. Instead of resisting my students, I accepted them, joining with them to help them learn, however they showed up. As I did so, they gradually became more receptive toward me. It wasn't an overnight turnaround, but in the weeks and months that followed, teaching them became easier.

Judging my students for not living up to how I thought they *should* be meant that I was essentially holding the shape of a box in my mind that circumscribed what I thought they should be like, how I thought they should act, and then insisting they assume the shape of my box. When they didn't, I looked down on them. I call this trying to fit someone or something into a "box of should." People can sense when someone else is trying to squeeze them into a box of should. They feel judged. They feel controlled. It pushes them out of their best selves and brings up their resistance.

Radical acceptance helped me turn my class into an oasis of acceptance and belonging. My students benefited because they felt accepted for who they were. I benefited because I was no longer wasting my energy arguing with reality.

To be clear, adopting a posture of radical acceptance didn't mean that I started allowing intolerable behaviors. Sometimes students bring unacceptable behaviors into our classrooms: disrespect, racism, homophobia, misogyny, harassment, bullying. To allow any of these behaviors in my classroom would undermine the learning environment and be antithetical to what I stand for. When even a hint of any of these behaviors shows up in my classroom, I vigorously respond to put a stop to them. But to avoid losing my best self in the process, I first have to accept the fact of what is happening. From this foundation of acceptance, I can appropriately respond from my best self.

Teachers know what it feels like to be put into a box of should because we often work under pressure to fit inside such a box—a box that dictates all the things we should be able to do and how well we should be able to do them. It's easy to internalize the boxes of should that other people have for us. This invariably leads to internal conflict, as some parts of ourselves resist the box, while other parts attempt to win approval by torquing ourselves to fit into the box, driving us to work late and on weekends, often at the cost of our well-being.

While it is not in our sphere of control to stop others from trying to make us fit into their boxes of should, we don't need to internalize those boxes; we don't need to attach our self-worth to whether we live up to someone else's idea of what a good teacher should be.

Human beings need to experience acceptance for who they are in order to have the best shot at fulfilling the promise within them. For students who spend each day dealing with teachers who are trying to make them fit inside a box of should, school becomes a lousy place. So also, for teachers who work inside a system that is trying to make them conform to an unrealistic box of should, school becomes a lousy place.

Ultimately, the most important person for us to radically accept is ourself. This means radically accepting our flaws, foibles, and limitations. It means accepting the burdens that come with living this life in these times, under these conditions. It means extending acceptance to our own mistake-prone, imperfect self while making room for sparks of magnificence that wait inside us, like buried treasure, to be discovered and expressed.

Radical acceptance of my body and the host of symptoms that came with chronic fatigue syndrome allowed me to come through the darkness, transmuting that misery into a blessing. For years, I heartily resisted the fact of being ill. I hated it. I hardened myself against it, even hating my own body and putting it into a box of should. My resistance did nothing but drain what little energy I had. It was only after I began accepting the fact of my illness and making peace with my body that I began to build up enough energy to heal. Radical acceptance helped me get well, but, more importantly, it made me a better, more resilient person. When I brought radical acceptance to my classroom, it made me a better, more resilient teacher.

 **REFLECTION QUESTIONS**

*Grab a notebook and something to write with and respond to the following questions:*

1 What is something that comes up for you as a teacher that you have a difficult time accepting?
2 What is the cost for you of resisting rather than accepting it?
3 Think of a time when someone tried to fit you inside of a box of should. What was that like? How did it feel?

# 12

# Choose *Yes*

When best applied, radical acceptance becomes a frame of mind that helps us to meet the ups and downs of life rather than resist them. A related idea is choosing *Yes. Yes* applied to education may seem counterintuitive. In fact, one of the most common bits of advice offered to new teachers is to learn to say "no." On the surface, learning to say "no" sounds like good advice. From the moment a teacher enters the profession, she faces one of teaching's greatest challenges: too much to do. The demands exceed her capacity to meet them in the time she has, but she wants to do well, so she's prone to say yes to additional responsibilities—yes to committees, yes to chaperoning dances, yes to being a club advisor—until her already-heaped plate is overflowing with tasks. This is how teachers become broken, so learning to say "no" appears to be a reasonable strategy. However, what it means to say "yes" or "no" deserves a second look, as deeper factors are at play.

As mentioned in Chapter 9, teaching from our best self entails making choices from a place of internal cohesion, a state where all the aspects making up our internal village are aligned and organized. Although saying "no" can save us from adding to the frenzy of too much to do, it doesn't help us become internally unified. We could say "no" and still be internally conflicted, which would make our decision stressful, costing us energy. Internally aligned choice is what we're after, and simply saying "no" won't help us get there. *Yes* is a much better approach.

DOI: 10.4324/9781003360513-15

There is a difference between "yes" and what I'm referring to as *Yes*. Ordinary "yes" is to verbally agree, to assent, to go along with. *Yes* is a force of nature; it's the "barbaric yawp" that Walt Whitman sounded over the roofs of the world (1855). We are moved by *Yes* when we are drawn to pet a puppy or soothe a crying baby. We can feel *Yes* moving in us as we listen to a favorite song. *Yes* draws us toward someone we are attracted to, electrifying us in the early days of a budding romance.

*Yes* helps us become our best self, even in high-stress, high-danger situations. It spurs firefighters to run into burning buildings, moved by the *Yes* to save someone's life. It emboldens the soldier running into gunfire to drag a fallen comrade to safety. When we see others act from *Yes*, we are inspired because we see through their actions the best of ourselves reflected back to us. *Yes* makes heroes of us. On the grandest scale, *Yes* may be the fundamental force in the universe driving all of creation. When we align ourselves with it, we move powerfully and frictionlessly, carried by *Yes* in the direction toward what we love.

*No*, on the other hand, repels us from what we detest or what we fear. From *No* we tense up, close down, push experience away.

At our most essential nature, we are each encoded, uniquely and particularly, with a fingerprint of things that, for no practical reason, we deeply love. When we move from those deep loves, our various villagers unite around our actions as surely as iron filings line up along a magnetized line. Internal conflict disappears, and our motion becomes relatively effortless because *Yes* draws us along.

I discovered the power of *Yes* through my struggle to get up in the morning. Though I had recovered from chronic fatigue enough to hold down my teaching job, getting out of bed remained an excruciating ordeal. Every morning, after my alarm went off, the first thing in my conscious awareness was how absolutely dead I felt. No matter how much sleep I had gotten, my body upon waking felt drained and impossibly heavy. Nothing in me wanted to move. I was filled with *No* for getting up. To get ready for work, I had to will myself, overriding the part of myself that hated the idea of getting out of bed. The energy consumed by that approach was enormous.

Once I had learned about *Yes*, I tried a different approach. After the alarm rang, I would lie there and think about the day ahead, scanning for something to look forward to, something that would spark *Yes*. Once I found it, I would hold the image of the activity or person or moment in my mind and let it draw me out of bed. This simple step conserved the energy that otherwise would have gone into battling myself. Not only was it easier to get up in the morning; my body could use the energy I had saved to heal.

Inspired, I began applying *Yes* to other situations. When I didn't want to do the dishes, rather than guilting myself into doing them, I would pause until I found a *Yes* for a clean kitchen. In the classroom, a *No* would rise up whenever I thought about grading. It felt like drudgery, so I would put it off until the pressure built up and my *No* for being a bad teacher who wasn't returning work to students became greater than my *No* for grading. Now I looked for a *Yes*—perhaps finding a *Yes* for the possibility of discovering something new about my students or a *Yes* for the satisfaction of being caught up.

Still, in the barrage of split-second decisions to be made during a typical teaching day, I often didn't have time to search for a *Yes*. I would forget about *Yes* and automatically react from *No*. A student entering the classroom late for the third time that week, another student listening to music while I was teaching, an email from an administrator introducing a new policy that teachers must submit their lesson plans a week ahead—before I could register what was happening, I would be far down the track of *No*.

It was karate training that offered a clue about how to transition to *Yes* in moments like these. Karate is fundamentally a set of techniques categorized as strikes (attacking movements), blocks (defensive movements), and stances (the structural support). As I mentioned in Chapter 1, trying to deal with a flurry of punches and kicks would make me tense, just as trying to deal with a flurry of things coming at me in the classroom would make me tense. A big part why I was tense had to do with *No*.

*No* tends to disconnect us from our best and, in so doing, foments our internal village to segregate into factions, each resisting something different. In the dojo, when I was sparring from *No*, some of my inner villagers would be trying to avoid humiliation. Some would be trying not to get hurt. Some would not want to disappoint my sensei, while others would be trying to win. With all of them pulling in different directions, I was reacting to my opponent from an internally conflicted place. The resulting *No* created tension and fear that made me prone to flail reactively rather than use the karate skills I had learned.

I needed a way to get to *Yes* when suddenly faced with an undesirable situation that demanded an immediate response. One day, Sensei Tom Spellman gave me the key. He told me that the Japanese word translated into English as "block" is *uke*. In Japanese, *uke* doesn't mean "block"; it means "receive." This idea radically shifted my mindset when it came to sparring in the dojo. The word "block" conjured a posture of *No*—something is coming at me, and I must resist and repel it with a blocking motion. But *uke* was about accepting the opponent's action and receiving it, a half-step toward *Yes*.

Receiving is a different mindset from blocking. While blocking puts me in resistance, receiving sets me up to respond with *Yes* to whatever is coming. From this mindset, blocks are no longer blocks; they are motions through which I receive and creatively redirect an attack.

With a mindset of *uke*, my awareness relaxed; I could read my opponent, see openings and subtle cues. From this receptive mindset, it became easy to respond from *Yes*. After an hour or more of intense sparring from a mindset of *uke*, I'd return home more energized than when I started.

This dramatic shift in the dojo readily translated to the classroom. The multitude of demands, expectations, problems to solve coming at teachers is quite similar to my sparring experience of punches and kicks coming at me in rapid succession. In both situations, it's instinctual to become tense and react from *No*. The principle of *uke* can help educators reframe all the demands flying our way as things to receive, rather than resist. And that opens the door to respond from *Yes*.

Another model for receiving and responding from *Yes* comes from improvisational theater. The cardinal rule of improv is to say "yes and" to whatever a fellow actor offers. For instance, if another actor says "Here's my ride," from "yes and" you might begin pantomiming a car pulling up next to him.

A receiving mindset can help teachers get to *Yes*, which in turn allows them to flow with, rather than resist, situations that arise in the classroom. Here is an example. Just as all the students are seated, one student pipes up: "Mr. Schroder, can we do nothing today?" Instinctually, I think: *No, of course we're not going to do nothing—what a dumb question.* But then I remember *uke*. I receive the student's input, and I look for my *Yes*:

> Sure. Let's do nothing. Everyone sit completely still. No phones out, no doodling, no fidgeting in your seats. Do nothing but quietly breathe. See if you can do nothing without letting your mind wander. If it wanders, just bring it back to your breath. Let's see if we can do absolutely nothing but breathe for three minutes. I'll do it with you. I'm setting the timer.

The student who suggested doing nothing expected pushback. Instead, I'm all in, taking his request literally and using it to introduce the class to the practice of mindfulness.

On another occasion, while I'm teaching in front of the class, a student rolls her eyes in response to something I say. I feel disrespected, and a *No* spontaneously arises inside me. If I react from this *No* and reproach that student for disrespecting me and the lesson, I will potentially damage our relationship and imperil the learning environment. But what if I remember *uke* and respond from *Yes*?

> Oh my gosh, that was an awesome eyeroll. Would you mind doing that again? I don't think I can eyeroll that well. Show me how you do it.

Now the whole class is laughing, watching the exchange. The student is smiling, and though she demurs, some part of her has just been assured that she won't be judged or criticized in my class, so she relaxes. She is unlikely to roll her eyes at me again because she's a little uncomfortable being the center of attention, and the whole point of rolling her eyes was to get me to react. When I don't give her that, she's more inclined to release the posture of *No* that prompted the eyeroll and join the flow of *Yes* with me and the rest of the class. When I resume teaching, the classroom feels lighter; everyone's attention has bumped up a notch.

For this to work, I need to openly receive the fact of her eyeroll and then find a genuine *Yes* within myself for it. If even a small part of me comes from *No*, the same words would come across as sarcastic, undermining the student's sense of safety in the class.

Remembering *uke* and responding from *Yes* helps us tap into a resilient best self who can deal with whatever happens. The stresses and daily frustrations of teaching become less consequential. *Yes* helps us retain access to our whole brains, enabling us to read the room and creatively respond to whatever happens by either going with it or redirecting it. Students begin to see us as practically imperturbable, so they stop trying to get the better of us and tend toward relaxing into the flow of learning.

Let's imagine a tougher situation. In response to my asking a student to follow along in the textbook, he blurts out: "This class sucks. I hate it here." This kind of comment pushes all kinds of buttons for teachers. First, we put care into crafting lessons, which makes it easy for this remark to hurt our feelings. Second, the student just called us out in front of everyone for teaching a sucky class; understandably, we may feel defensive. One thing is certain: we suddenly have the full attention of every student in the class. How will the teacher handle this?

If I block him from *No* and counterattack, I might say: "I've had it with your disrespect. Get out of my classroom!" A *No*-based retort like that is likely to lead to a *No*-versus-*No* power struggle, escalating until I am frazzled and the student leaves the room angry, referral in hand.

However, if I remember *uke* and remember *Yes*, I receive what he's said and take a moment to look for my *Yes*. "Wow," I say,

> it must be tough coming to a class you hate. I understand you don't want to be here, so I appreciate that you came

today. I am curious if you'd be willing to help me make this a better class. How about you write down your ideas and turn them in at the end of the period? I'm looking for thoughtful ideas for the class, and if you give me those, I will give you credit in place of the assignment the rest of us are doing.

Then I turn from the student and go back to teaching the class.

Again, I need to be open and genuinely coming from *Yes* for this not to come across as sarcastic. I'm actually curious about what the student will write.

A response like that disarms the student. He might write up a list of ideas (which I am happy to receive and discuss with him). He might write a rant about what a terrible class this is (which can become a good way for him to learn how to use writing to express and release emotional content), or he might decide it's easier to let go of his *No* and join the class. Or he may simply sit there. In the rare case that the outbursts continue, I am happy to talk further in the hallway, but always from *Yes*. He still may end up with that referral, but more importantly, I won't become an upset mess. I will have retained my best self.

From *Yes*, I don't give students anything to oppose. If a student says he hates an assignment, I say, "Okay. What do you want to do instead?" I let him know what skills the assignment is designed to teach and then say, "Rather than this assignment, what would you like to do to demonstrate that you have learned these skills?"

Rarely do students come up with a suggestion. If they do, great; they've just opened up a way for me to help them connect their *Yes* to the work in class. But most of the time, students just want something to push against; they want to express some rebellion. *Yes* allows me to sidestep their resistance. From *Yes*, I am no longer in the space they thought they were pushing against. Instead, I've moved alongside them, and from a position of support, I am essentially saying, "Where do you want to go with your life? Wherever that is, if I can, I'll help you to get there."

**REFLECTION QUESTIONS**

*Grab a notebook and something to write with and respond to the following questions:*

1  Think of a moment in the classroom when you reacted from *No*. What was the situation, and what happened?
2  What is an example of something you've done that came from *Yes*? Describe that experience.
3  Consider this scenario: for the third time during a lesson, two students are having an audible side conversation while you are trying to teach. You know you need to address this. How might you do it from *No*? How might you do it from *Yes*?

# 13

# Saying "No" from *Yes*

After I learned how to meet situations from *Yes*, teaching began to be more fun. Still, I knew that I needed to say "no" sometimes. How could I do that and still come from *Yes*?

It turns out that teaching from *Yes* doesn't mean never saying "no." Whether we say "yes" or "no" matters little compared to which place—a deeper *Yes* or a deeper *No*—we say it from.

Let's say that an administrator asks a teacher to join a school improvement committee. It seems like the teacher has two options: he can say "yes" or "no." In reality, however, he has four. Let's say he says "yes" because he doesn't want the administrator to see him as someone not willing to go that extra mile for students. If he says "yes" for that reason, his "yes" is actually coming from a deeper *No* to the possibility of his administrator negatively judging him. He could also say "no" from a deeper *No*. For instance, he might turn down the request because he is afraid the committee work would consume his life.

He could also say "yes" from a deeper *Yes*, agreeing to join the committee from a *Yes* for the opportunity to contribute to the work of improving the students' experience at school. But—and this is important—he could also say "no" while coming from *Yes*. Perhaps that *Yes* is for time with his family or for that hour at the gym he's promised himself after work every day. Saying "no" from a *Yes* really means unchoosing one possibility in order to say *Yes* to something else.

DOI: 10.4324/9781003360513-16

To summarize the options, we can say:

| "yes" | from a deeper *No* | "Yes, I'll join the committee." Driven from fear of how the principal will see me if I don't say yes. |
|---|---|---|
| "no" | from a deeper *No* | "No, I won't join the committee." Driven from fear that the job will consume my personal life. |
| "yes" | from a deeper *Yes* | "Yes, I will join the committee." Driven by clarity about how the committee work connects with *Yes* for my deeper purpose. |
| "no" | from a deeper *Yes* | "No, I won't join the committee." Driven by my *Yes* for time with family or for something else I value. |

This might seem like parsing semantics, but whether we come from *No* or *Yes* turns out to matter a great deal. *Yes* prompts our internal aspects to pull together, allowing us to choose from an internally aligned state, while *No* engenders tension and internal conflict that wears us down.

One of the problems with choosing from *No* is that we can be haunted by internal conflict even after the choice has been made. For instance, if the teacher says "yes" to being on the committee from a *No* to the possibility of his administrator thinking less of him, as he sits in committee meetings, a part of him will still be invested in the desire to control how his supervisor sees him. This will leave him internally divided, with one part of him trying to be seen a particular way and another part wanting to contribute to the committee. In addition, he may begin resenting his time on the committee as another voice pipes up: *I should be at the gym right now.*

Saying "no" from *No* isn't much better. Although he won't be adding another task to his already-full plate, after making the decision, he is likely to second-guess himself with intrusive thoughts: *I should have agreed to the committee. I wonder what my principal thinks of me now. She probably thinks I don't care, that I'm not a team player.*

If, on the other hand, he says "no" to the committee from a *Yes* for that gym workout, he is liberated to immerse himself in that workout from an internal alignment that comes from *Yes*.

Likewise, if he says "yes" to the committee from *Yes* because he believes in the committee's work and is inspired to be a part of it, he is essentially unchoosing the time at the gym because this committee appears to be the choice that better reflects his deepest values. When he shows up to the meetings from this kind of *Yes*, he is internally aligned and ready to get to work. If, after a meeting or two, he recognizes the committee isn't what he thought it would be, he can change his choice in favor of his *Yes* for that daily workout. The machines, the free weights, that gym smell is calling.

Coming from *Yes* frees us to say "no" to our students as well. For instance, if a student asks me, "Mr. Schroder, can we go outside today?" I remember *uke* and receive what she said, consider the lesson, consider the additional distractions being outside would bring, consider any technology needs, and consider my intentions (my *Yes*) for the lesson. Having considered all these factors, I may say, "No, today isn't a good day for that." I'm saying "no," but I'm coming from a place of *Yes* to deliver the best lesson I can, the lesson that offers maximum benefit to my students at a minimum cost to me.

Whether we say "yes" or "no" matters less than whether we are connected to our genuine *Yes*, inspiring our internal village of aspects to join together around a common cause. When they are aligned, we can move through our day with clarity, passion, and an open heart.

 **REFLECTION QUESTIONS**

*Grab a notebook and something to write with and respond to the following questions:*

1   Imagine that an administrator has just asked if you would take on an extra duty as a club advisor. In your writing, explore the thoughts and feelings that would arise in you if you were to say:
  • "yes" from a deeper *No*
  • "no" from a deeper *No*
  • "yes" from a deeper *Yes*
  • "no" from a deeper *Yes*.

# 14

# Classroom Management

## Know Your Prime Directive

Applying *Yes* can be confusing when dealing with disruptive students. What does *Yes* look like when a student is interrupting the lesson or clowning around to draw the class's attention off the lesson and onto himself? What about when other students join in and the lesson is completely derailed?

Questions like these get at the heart of classroom management, one of most challenging aspects of teaching to master. One reason it is so hard is that classroom management issues can cue us to become internally conflicted. This was my problem as a new teacher. On the one hand, I didn't want to be a strict, authoritarian teacher; on the other hand, I wanted my classes to run smoothly. Not knowing how to reconcile these conflicting drives, I would at times be too lenient and at times too strict, making me ineffectual. The stress of this took a toll on both my physical and mental health.

During my first year of teaching, an administrator on the brink of retirement gave me a classroom management pep talk; he shared a story about an army officer who dealt with the problem of unruly troops by shooting one of the offenders in the presence of the other soldiers. "After that," the administrator explained, "the army officer had no more trouble." Then the administrator

DOI: 10.4324/9781003360513-17

looked me in the eye and said, "Sometimes you have to shoot one."

I knew he was speaking metaphorically, but what would it mean to "shoot one"? The pep talk wasn't helpful. Still, it made me think about the kind of teacher I wanted to be.

Months later, after delivering another awful teaching performance, I sat at my desk and started reflectively writing about the problems I was having with disruptive students. As I wrote, I recalled something Paul Richards had told me. Like many things Paul said to me, it was spoken casually, just slipped into the conversation. "It's good," he had said, "to have a reason for everything you do, a reason that flows from a single overarching *Yes*." I wondered what an overarching *Yes*—for making choices around classroom management—might be. That's when I thought of *Star Trek*.

In the world of *Star Trek*, Starfleet is guided by a baseline policy called the Prime Directive. In the television series and subsequent films, Starfleet's Prime Directive is that, as crews explore the universe, they are never to do anything that could interfere with the natural development of an alien civilization. *Enterprise* crew members are duty-bound to elevate the Prime Directive over all other considerations, even the survival of the ship and everyone on board. The creators of *Star Trek* used the Prime Directive for dramatic purposes. I realized I could use this concept to help me manage my classroom.

That afternoon, on a page in a spiral notebook, I wrote: "My Prime Directive is to protect and safeguard the learning environment, to maximize every student's ability to learn." Now I was clear. I would swiftly and firmly deal with any student behavior that disrupted the learning environment or my ability to be effective within it. My primary concern wouldn't be the troublemakers; it would be the other students in the class. Every bit of me could line up around this *Yes*.

The next day, a student gave me an opportunity to apply my Prime Directive by interrupting a discussion to ask if I got high and then pantomiming someone taking a preposterously deep drag on a joint. Of course, the whole class erupted into laughter. Prior to this, I would have become flustered. In the turmoil of my own internal conflict, I might have overreacted, or I might have tried to laugh it off while quietly seething. Neither response would have been effective.

This time, without raising my voice, I asked the student to step outside the room. Then I continued the lesson with the rest of the class. When we got to a portion of the lesson that involved independent work, I stepped into the hallway, where the student was waiting. After a brief chat in which I made my expectations clear, I sent him to the disciplinarian's office with a referral in hand. Simple. Undramatic. The student had negatively impacted the learning environment in my classroom, so I dealt with it in a way that least impacted the rest of the class. My Prime Directive gave me the clarity to manage my classroom from my best self.

That you have a Prime Directive matters more than what Prime Directive you choose. However, my Prime Directive has served me well for over 20 years, so you're welcome to appropriate it as your own.

My Prime Directive gives me a single preeminent *Yes*. It tells me what matters, and it simplifies classroom management down to one question: Is this behavior threatening or damaging to the learning space or my ability to be effective within it? From this one question, I can be clear and consistent with every classroom management choice while cultivating a learning environment that supports both me and my students to be at our best.

 **REFLECTION QUESTIONS**

*Grab a notebook and something to write with and respond to the following questions:*

1   Use reflective writing to find your way to a Prime Directive that all of you can line up behind.
2   Think of a situation you have found problematic. Given your new Prime Directive, how will you respond to that situation going forward?

# 15

# Developing Field-Based Attention as an Antidote to Mental Fatigue

On many days, after the final bell and the students had left, I would slump at my desk, idly wishing for a job in which I could pay attention to one thing at a time. How glorious it would be, I thought, to be a therapist seeing only one patient at a time, or a surgeon operating on just one knee, or a pilot flying only one airplane. Any job that required a single focus, especially single focus in an environment with minimal distraction, would be like an elixir to my exhausted brain.

The only time I was free to pay attention to one thing was during my prep period, when I would be grading student work or planning lessons. The rest of the day, I was caught in a ceaseless multidirectional tug of war for my attention: various district mandates to implement, multiple standards to teach to, 30 or more students all simultaneously wanting or needing something, a mob of emails gathering in my inbox.

I would marvel at how tired my attention would become, how much easier it was to focus before lunch. By afternoon, I would have to push myself to do what had been effortless just a few hours earlier. By day's end, my attention would be zapped. I'd go home and collapse in front of a mindless show on television.

After years of this, one day, while feeling particularly used up, I got online and googled the words "attention fatigue."

DOI: 10.4324/9781003360513-18

I wanted to know if there was such a thing. That's when I learned about a neuropsychological condition called Directed Attention Fatigue (DAF).

DAF is a condition in which the brain becomes fatigued from a person's efforts to focus their attention in a high-stimulus environment. To allow us to pay attention in a distractive environment, the brain employs inhibitory mechanisms that suppress the distractions. These mechanisms are quick to tire. As they wear down, the brain's capacity to maintain focus is rapidly exhausted, leading to DAF. Symptoms of DAF include irritability, impatience, reduced ability to perform regular tasks, less sensitivity to social cues, impaired judgment, and increased distractibility (*Directed Attention Fatigue—Wikidoc*, n.d.). This pretty much described what I had been experiencing late in the teaching day.

According to research, DAF can be alleviated through spending time in nature, getting more and better sleep, removing clutter from your surroundings, meditation, and taking breaks. Visiting a natural area ("urban environments tend to be poor environments for restoring directed attention") or meditating can help (Kaplan & Berman, 2010). However, other than a brief respite at lunch, a teacher's attention has to be "on" from the moment students arrive at school until they get on the buses to go home. There isn't time in a teacher's day to implement these DAF-reducing strategies.

In addition to DAF, teachers also suffer from mental fatigue, caused by switching the focus of attention from person to person and thing to thing. Research on multitasking (which in fact is research on people switching their attention from one task to another in rapid succession) has shown that shifting attention from one thing to something else consumes oxygenated glucose in the brain, leaving the person mentally tired, compromising both cognitive and physical performance (Levitin, 2015).

It turns out that we can prevent afternoon mental fatigue and DAF crashes. The secret lies in how we pay attention.

We know that we can choose what we pay attention to. We can direct our attention toward a student or a passage in a book, or we can look out the window and attend to a bird on a branch.

But this isn't the only attention choice we have. We can also choose the shape our attention takes.

For instance, we can focus our attention like a laser beam and zero in on that bird. When we do this, our world constricts to bird size. In the Western world, this way of using attention is celebrated. We tell our students to focus, to concentrate, directing them to compress their attention down to a vector focused on one math problem or one passage in a textbook. Learning to perform a task well often requires mastering this concentrated, vector-style attention. Most of us learn this attention approach in childhood and it becomes habitual.

You might notice how vector-style attention works at a gathering such as a cocktail party. You are talking with one person when the host comes over and introduces you to someone else. If you are in vector-style attention, the person you have been talking to disappears from your awareness as your attention shifts to the host and the new person.

Vector-style attention forces our brains to suppress surrounding distractions and shift our vector attention from one thing to the next, making us susceptible to both DAF and mental fatigue, wearing us down through the course of a day, and cumulatively depleting us through the school year. But we don't have to use our attention in this pinpointed way.

It is also possible to relax our attention, letting it take the form of a field that encompasses everything within that field. When looking at that bird out the window with a field-style attention, we not only take in the bird but also the blue sky behind it, the other birds nearby, and the tree the bird is perched in. Within our attention field, we can highlight the bird as the center of our focus while still attending to the whole scene. This way, we can access the advantages of field-style attention while still maintaining a central focal point.

The advantages of using our attention as a field are many. For one, this style of attention is relaxing. Think of the last time you went to the beach and watched the waves roll in or watched the sunset. These were replenishing moments in part because such scenes cue our attention to take the form of a large, expansive field. Allowing our attention to take the shape of a field also makes us less susceptible to DAF because everything in our surroundings is, by definition, included in that field, so our brain doesn't have to work to filter out distractions. And when our attention encompasses our surroundings, we don't need to continually shift our attention from person to person and thing to thing, which reduces mental fatigue.

When looking out a window at an unobstructed view, our attention tends to automatically shift into the shape of a field to take in the whole vista. However, it isn't necessary to look out a window or sit on a hilltop to benefit from field-style attention. We can choose the shape of our attention, whether a field or a laser beam, in any setting. At that cocktail party, it's possible for you to expand your attention to include both the person you are speaking with and the host and the new person she wants to introduce you to.

Interestingly, you can include someone or something in your field of attention even when you are not looking at them, since attention does not require vision. For instance, when your conversation with the first person is interrupted and you turn to look at the second person, your attention field can still include the first person. We can attend to what we hear, what we smell or taste, what we think, and we can attend to someone walking up behind us. We can also change the size of our field of attention, expanding or shrinking it to whatever size best suits the situation. When lying on our back in the grass during a meteor shower at night, we may expand our field of attention to take in the entire night sky.

The capacity to deploy our attention as a field is a huge boon for classroom teachers. Let your attention fill your classroom, then highlight a central reference point within that space. What you've highlighted becomes the center of focus within your attention field.

With my attention in the form of a classroom-sized field, when Darian asks a question, rather than laser-beaming my attention onto him, I simply shift the central reference point to Darian. My field of attention stays the same; I'm simply shifting the focal point within it. Once my exchange with Darian is finished, I can move the central reference point to another student or to a passage in a book we are reading, all while maintaining my attention in the shape of a classroom-sized field.

A big advantage to field-shaped attention in the classroom is that it makes classroom management easier. While Darian is asking his question, I can be simultaneously aware of the fact that Maria, on the other side of the room, is sneakily texting and that something is up with Eric, who is uncharacteristically slouched at his desk. I can detect classroom management issues when they are small and easy to address. Student blow-ups aren't typically spun from thin air. There are usually subtle clues ahead of time, precursors that are visible to a teacher whose attention operates as a field.

Shifting a habit of attention takes a bit of effort. If, like most of us, your attention is conditioned to the laser-beam style, it will automatically lock onto the individual or thing you are directing it toward. You'll want to recognize when that's happening, while also reminding yourself that you can make a different choice.

Try it now as you're reading this book. It's likely that you have a laser-like focus on what you are reading. Let's start with that. Let your attention concentrate on just these words while everything else disappears.

Now, shift to field-style attention. Expand your attention to include your surroundings while highlighting the words in this sentence as the central focal point. Be careful that you aren't simply switching a laser-like attention between the book and other elements in the room. Instead, allow your attention to form a field that contains this book, the space in the room, and the objects within it.

Because your field of attention need not be married to the direction of your visual gaze, you can allow your attention to include what is below you, above you, and behind you. Include the sensation of being seated in a chair while keeping the central focus on these words and the thoughts and images they evoke in your mind as you read.

To help you experience the difference between your attention as a field and as a vector, return to an exclusive laser-like focus on these words. Focus your attention even more tightly on each word. Then allow your attention to relax out into a field shape again.

Taking a few minutes every day to practice shifting from laser to field attention will help you repattern your attention habits. In time, field-based attention will become natural, and you won't even have to think about it. Remembering to use your attention as a field rather than a vector offers an extremely high ROI. It can be a career saver, and a mental health saver. It has been for me.

 **REFLECTION QUESTIONS**

*Grab a notebook and something to write with and respond to the following questions:*

1   To what degree do you suffer from DAF and/or mental fatigue as the teaching day wears on?
2   What did you notice as you practiced shifting your attention from a vector to a field while reading this chapter?

# 16

# The Curiously Nourishing Power of Attention

Once I learned to bring a field of attention to my classroom, I experienced less mental fatigue and could more easily focus in the afternoons. However, I still had more to learn about attention.

I had always thought that my attention was primarily for me—a tool for gaining knowledge, developing a skill, or performing a task. This isn't entirely wrong. Paying attention is a necessary part of doing a complex action. But one day, Paul Richards upended this conventional understanding of attention and showed me how my attention could support my students in bringing their best selves to my classroom.

Paul and I met at a favorite walking trail that runs parallel to a creek in a local park. Above our heads, the leaves of oaks and broadleaf maples stirred as we walked in their shade. At the time, I was struggling with a number of issues. My health was still poor, and I was sleeping most weekends to recover from teaching. While under this much strain, as well as caught in a confusing tangle of unidentified hurtspots, my marriage was crumbling. Trying to live on my teacher's salary, we were barely scraping by.

Paul asked me how I was doing. I told him and then asked, "Given the struggles I'm facing, what do you think would be most helpful for me to put my attention on right now?"

DOI: 10.4324/9781003360513-19

He paused. The creek flowed on. The shadows of moving leaves dappled the path in front of us.

"We think," he began, "that we change by paying attention to ourselves and that we solve problems by focusing our attention on them. But this is a misunderstanding of what attention is for. The highest purpose of our attention is not to help ourselves; it's to nourish and change others."

"But surely," I said, "I am improving at karate because of my attention on it."

"Training is important, but your improvement has quite a bit to do with the attention you receive from your karate sensei."

As we walked along the creek, Paul continued: "If you were rowing a boat up this creek, your back would be facing where you are going, and you would be facing what's coming along behind you. Life is like that. We pay attention to the people coming up behind us, and the people ahead of us pay attention to us. This is how mentorships work and how skills like martial arts are passed from sensei to student in a chain that stretches for generations. We grow through the attention of those beyond us."

Until that moment, I had assumed my students were improving because of their attention on the lessons. However, I realized, I was also paying attention to them. Through interacting with them, guiding them, being curious about them and their learning styles, through developing curriculum with them in mind and offering feedback on their work, I was giving them my attention. Could my attention on them be playing a larger role in learning than I thought? I wondered what would happen if I was more intentional about the way I paid attention.

Now, after two decades of experimenting with being deliberate about paying attention to my students, it is clear to me that my attention is the greatest resource I have for inspiring students to bring their best selves to class and my best tool for helping them awaken their potential.

To appreciate the massive impact of our attention on someone, especially on a young person, consider what happens when that attention is absent. In the 1980s, Romania's Communist dictator Nicolae Ceausescu wanted to increase Romania's population to spark the economy, so he curtailed the availability of contraception, imposed tax penalties on people who were child-less, and celebrated "heroine mothers" who gave birth to ten or more children. For parents who were unable to take care of all their children, he promoted a national campaign with the slogan "The state can take care of your child better than you can."

By the time Ceausescu was ousted from power in 1989, an estimated 170,000 infants and children were living in state-run orphanages. Images and videos taken inside these orphanages are chilling examples of child neglect. Charles Nelson, professor of pediatrics at Harvard Medical School, describes walking into an orphanage in Bucharest to see a small child standing there sobbing. According to Nelson, the child:

> was heartbroken and had wet his pants. I asked, "What's going on with that child?" A worker said, "Well, his mother abandoned him this morning, and he's been like that all day." That was it. No one comforted the little boy or picked him up.
>
> (Fay Greene, 2020)

In 2000, Nelson gained permission to conduct a study with 136 of the institutionalized children (ages 6 months to 3 years). Under the conditions of the study, called the Bucharest Intervention Project, half the children continued to receive "care as usual" in the orphanage, and half were placed with foster care families whom the researchers had recruited and trained. Local parents volunteered their kids to make up the control group. After tracking the children's development for years, Nelson and his team found that the children living in the attention-starved environment of the orphanage "had delays in cognitive function, motor development, and language. They also showed deficits in socio-emotional behaviors and experienced more psychiatric disorders" (Weir, 2014). Meanwhile, the children assigned to fos-ter parents showed dramatic improvements in language, IQ, and social-emotional functioning. Although the children in foster homes were still significantly behind the control group of kids who had never been institutionalized, it was clear that some-thing beneficial for the children was happening in foster families that wasn't happening in the orphanage. The physical needs—food, clothing, warmth, shelter—of both groups were being met. However, unlike the children in foster care, the children in the orphanages were starved of attention.

Child psychologists use this study to point to the devastating effect that neglect has on child development, theorizing that attachment is a biological imperative. And what is the precursor to attachment? Love and affection, yes. But even more fundamental is attention. Attention is the precursor to love. We must give our attention to someone before we can love them, and then within that loving attention, attachment develops. According to Nelson, without a reliable source of attention, affection, and stimulation, "the wiring of the brain goes awry" (Hamilton, 2014). The conditions in those orphanages demonstrated that while food, clothing, and a place to sleep are vital to a child's development, caring attention is just as indispensable. Attention is so crucial to the development of neural pathways in the brains of children that it actually affects brain volume; the brains of the control group were actually larger than the brains of the institutionalized children (Weir, 2014).

In schools around the country, it's common to hear a teacher say about a difficult student: "He's just trying to get attention." Well, of course he is. As the Bucharest study demonstrates, the brains and bodies of children starve when deprived of attention. Starving people will resort to whatever means necessary to get what they need. We wouldn't say about a hungry child: "He's just trying to get you to feed him." Attention-deprived young people will naturally try to get attention however they can. When one is starving for attention, even negative attention is better than no attention at all.

How much attention does a student need to feel nourished? The answer varies from student to student, and a student starving for attention will require more, but in general, the quantity of attention matters less than the quality. A little dose of undivided attention is enough for most students to feel nourished in a class.

Under the pressures of the job, teachers are prone to be preoccupied by all the things they need to do, so when they do give a student attention, it's often the minimum required to get the student on the right page in the workbook or to help them answer a question. But for our attention to really benefit someone, we need to be as present as possible with them; we can't attempt to "be efficient" and multitask. We can't be absorbed in thinking about all the things we need to do.

It yields a high ROI to offer each student our full attention at some point every day, freely giving that attention from *Yes*, as internally unified within ourselves as possible. One of the best practices I have found for this is to greet each student individually at the start of class. At some schools, teachers are instructed to stand at the door and greet students as they enter the classroom. That is good if you can make it work, but I have found that as class time approaches, students tend to arrive in clumps, making it impossible to attend fully to each student. So I typically wait until they are in the room. Some days I go around student by student, fist bumping, saying hello, asking about their day, complimenting a new haircut or a new pair of shoes. But to avoid making it too formalized, on other days I welcome each student from the front of the room as they enter. As the class gets underway, I keep the importance of my attention in mind, responding to student comments and questions with undivided attention.

Another method I use to give students my attention has the additional benefit of increasing the ROI of grading. I do much of my grading while students are in the room, calling them up to my desk to discuss their work and involving them in the grading process. With longer writing assignments, I preview student work ahead of time, making notes in the margins. These notes are more for me than for my students, helping me remember what I want to say. When I'm ready to grade, I'll get the class quietly working and call each student to my desk. This one-on-one attention helps students grow as thinkers and learners much more than if I graded student work alone.

If the work doesn't yet meet a standard, or if I think a student didn't bring to bear their best effort, I will tell them what they need to redo or revise. High school students notoriously hate to redo their assignments, but when I give a student my full attention, making sure they know exactly what I am looking for on the next draft, they often actually thank me before returning to their desk and getting to work on the rewrite.

One caveat to this process of meeting with students one-on-one to discuss their work is that it only works when I maintain a field-based attention that encompasses the whole classroom while I'm working with an individual student. If my attention field collapses to a vector, or even to a small field encompassing only the student I am working with, the rest of the class will go off task, and I have to pause the conference to get back up in front of the room and refocus the class. But if I maintain a field of attention in the room, as implausible as it might sound, students tend to quietly work, which frees me up to meet with individual students at my desk.

Giving students regular doses of undivided attention helps bring out their best selves. The small amount of time invested is well worth it. When students bring their best, they are more receptive to the lessons, which makes the job of teaching them considerably easier.

 **REFLECTION QUESTION**

*Grab a notebook and something to write with and respond to the following question:*

1   What are some ways you can take advantage of the power of attention to nourish your students and support them to bring their best selves to your classroom?

# 17

# The Vital Role of Positive Messages

Students do better in learning environments in which they are validated, appreciated, and feel cared for. One of the best ways to create that kind of classroom environment is through giving students positive messages.

By "positive message," I'm not talking about empty praise or compliments. I don't mean gold stars, smiley stickers, or participation ribbons. I'm talking about bringing curious attention to another person and then being moved to speak in a manner that highlights something positive about them. A positive message is a way to deliver a package of nourishing attention, wrapped in words and actions, to another human being.

Research shows that reflecting the positives we see in someone is one of the best ways to help them access their best selves. In one study, research subjects asked friends, relatives, and coworkers to write about the subject's strengths. After reading these narratives rich in positive messages, the subjects showed measurable improvements in performance, better immune responses, a 200% improvement in creative problem solving, and significantly less anxiety (Cable, 2019, p. 63). Further research demonstrated that telling someone about their strengths boosts both physical and mental functioning and enhances motivation for growth and learning.

DOI: 10.4324/9781003360513-20

One reason positive messages are so powerful is that the self we identify with, and that we believe is us, is really nothing more than a story we tell ourselves (Cable, 2019, p. 59). This story shapes how we act and how others respond to us. When someone gives us a positive message, we can use it to upgrade our story. When we upgrade our story, we change the way we see ourselves and our abilities.

In the absence of receiving positive messages from others, human beings tend to focus on problems—problems in their environment, and problems in themselves. This is because the brain gives more weight to negative information than to positive. Scientists call this "negativity bias." It's part of the same survival adaptation that kept our early ancestors on the lookout for threats. Those threats could be external or internal; to gain a survival advantage, humans evolved to fixate on problems.

Though focusing on negatives helped our ancestors survive, doing so doesn't help modern humans become fulfilled. In fact, focusing on our own shortcomings drives us toward depression, anxiety, and an acute susceptibility to stress reactions (Williams et al., 2009). One of the best ways to break our fixation on our weaknesses is to receive positive messages from others.

As discussed in Chapter 10, we want our students' seeking systems to be activated. Receiving positive messages tends to awaken a person's seeking system, energizing and motivating them to more deeply engage with their work (Cable, 2019, p. 61). When the seeking system is activated, the brain releases dopamine, which increases motivation and makes people feel more zestful, purposeful, and alive. They become motivated to learn, to explore, to create meaning.

Every educator faces the challenge of how to motivate students. One common approach is to use extrinsic rewards, such as treats, privileges, or stickers. But rather than providing long-term motivation, this practice weakens students' seeking systems. Instead of releasing dopamine, extrinsic rewards release natural opioids, which puts people into a contented stupor (Cable, 2019, p. 23). Threats of punishment are even worse, awakening students' fear systems, making them anxious and wary, and leading them down the path toward stress reactions, resistance, and disengagement (Cable, 2019, p. 8).

Giving positive messages is an efficient way to give nourishing attention to our students while activating their seeking systems. The better we become at giving messages, the more positive influence we can have on our students' growth and learning.

After years of experimenting with positive messages in the classroom, I've identified the following seven as the most important messages students need to hear from teachers:

1. *I see you.*

   "I see you" is the fundamental positive message. People need to feel seen before they will accept any other message. Seeing something positive in a student, naming it, and affirming it helps that student integrate that positive attribute into their own story about themselves. To effectively deliver this message, we need to pay attention, notice the student's strengths, and then appropriately express what we see.

   To give this message, I typically don't say the words, "I see you." Instead, I see something positive about the student, and simply report what I see. For instance, I might say,

   > Hey, Joel, I noticed you were frustrated earlier on this assignment. I don't know if this is true or not, but it looked to me like a part of you wanted to quit. But you didn't quit. You kept at it. And now you've finished, and you've done an excellent job.

   To deliver this message, I had to pay attention to Joel so I could reflect back what I saw.

2. *You are welcome here (I am happy to see you).*

   Everyone has a deep need to feel welcome, to feel that they belong, and to know that someone is happy to see them. One way we can convey this message is through how we greet students when they come through the door. When I see a student, I allow myself to feel my *Yes* for their presence and then let that *Yes* express through my words, tone of voice, and body language when I say, "Good morning, Isaiah!" or "Great to see you, Sarah!" It isn't dramatic; it's genuine.

Dogs are masters of enthusiastic welcomes. You come home after a long day at work, unlock the front door, and there is your dog, wiggling and barking with joy that you've arrived. It's a good feeling.

School would be a different kind of place if every student felt welcomed as they entered their classrooms.

3. *You're in the pack (you matter).*
This message is often delivered more powerfully in actions than in words. A phone call home to a student who hasn't been in class for a few days, just to check in and make sure everything is okay, conveys a powerful "You're in the pack" message.

Another way to deliver this message is through differentiating instruction and working individually with students who are struggling to help them succeed.

Back when I assigned lists of spelling words for students to learn, there was a student in one of my sophomore classes who consistently struggled with spelling. I would watch her study, even help her study, yet she failed test after test. She told me she was just a terrible speller, but I didn't let it go at that. I started being curious about her more generally and asked her what she liked to do. It turned out that she loved basketball and would practice shooting hoops for hours at home.

"Okay," I said, "I want you to go home and play horse tonight, using each word on this spelling list." Two days later, the class took the test. After grading her test, I called her up to my desk. "Look, you scored 100%."

She looked at the test, then at me, then back at the test. Her eyes filled with tears. "I thought I was dumb," she said, "but I see … I'm not."

Students need to feel that being part of a class means something. They need to feel that they personally matter and that the teacher will not leave them behind.

4. *I not only see you; I accept and validate what I see.*
To accept and validate someone means to make space for and affirm them exactly as they are. Although everyone needs to feel validated, this message seems particularly important for young people to receive from adults they trust.

It's easy to think we can give positive messages only when we catch a student doing something right, but positive messages can be woven into an interaction at any time. For example, let's say a student repeatedly arrives late for class. A teacher might to try to get the student to change his behavior by threatening punishment or by making a sarcastic comment such as, "Oh, look who decided to show up," leading the student to put up a defensive barrier that will leave him less receptive to learning.

The teacher will get better results by welcoming the student into her class, then later calling him up to her desk to talk about his lateness. In conversations like this, I often start with an observation and follow it up with something I want to validate. In this instance, I might say,

I've noticed this is the second time this week you've been late to class. I imagine it must be stressful coming in and not knowing what we're doing and having to catch up. Can you give me any insight on why you are late?

By acknowledging the discomfort of coming into the room and not knowing what process is underway, I am validating part of his experience. Then I listen to what the student has to say.

There are many reasons why a student might be late, but let's say he says something like this: "I have shop class right before this class, and the shop is on the other side of campus. Sometimes other students leave without putting their materials away, so I stay for a couple minutes and help Mr. Romero clean up."

A response like that gives me an opening to offer the student another message of validation:

> It says a lot about your character that you stop to help Mr. Romero. I admire that. Here's the thing, though. Your being late is becoming a problem because, first, it makes it harder for you to stay caught up in class, and second, you're breaking the school tardy policy, which is my job to enforce by writing tardy referrals. If you are late again, I need to write up one of those referrals. What solution do you propose?

I am making my expectation clear while couching it in a positive message about the student's character. I'm also letting him know the consequences if he continues to arrive late. And, instead of threatening him, I'm empowering him to solve the problem.

However the student responds to my initial question about why he is late, I can follow up with a message of validation. He might say, "Because I don't like rushing— it stresses me out," or "Because I hate this class, and I don't want to be here." To that, I can say,

> I get it. When I was in high school, there were classes I didn't want to go to either. Sorry you're having that experience with this class. Is there something I can do to help you hate this class a little less?

Because the student is receiving acceptance and validation, even if he is unable to solve the problem and I end up writing that referral, the relationship between us will likely remain solid, and the student will be more apt to bring his best self to class.

5. *I expect your best.*
   Too often, teachers assume they must choose between being stern and holding high expectations for student performance and being warm and accepting while letting

half-baked work slide. But having a warm demeanor and holding high expectations are not mutually exclusive. In her book *Culturally Responsive Teaching and the Brain*, Zarretta Hammond (2015) references the kind of teacher who is "a warm demander," meaning the teacher embodies a combination of "personal warmth and active demandingness" while pushing students to stretch beyond their comfort zone (pp. 97–98). We can all be warm demanders, which is exactly what our students need.

The message of "I expect your best" is another message that is well expressed through both words and actions rather than words alone. Although I tell my students that I expect their best, they may not really get the message until I ask them to redo a rushed-through, carelessly done assignment. Giving students the message of high expectations lets them know that we take them, their work, and their education seriously.

6. *I am for you (I have confidence in you).*
   Young people need to know that their teachers believe in them and are behind them. When a teacher stands in her *Yes* for a student—for that student's potential, for the person that student can become—and expresses her stance through words and actions, the student is much more likely to want to succeed in that teacher's class.

   As discussed in Chapter 5, even under the best conditions, the process of learning is frustrating. To get through the frustration at stage 2, and experience success, students need reassurance and encouragement from someone they trust and respect, someone who is saying, "I know this is difficult right now, but you can do it. I believe in you."

7. *You are safe.*
   Keeping students physically safe is a given, but to awaken their best selves, their sense of being socially, emotionally, and psychologically safe is just as important. Bessel Van Der Kolk, one of the world's foremost authorities on how the brain adapts to trauma, writes: "Being

able to feel safe with others is probably the single most important aspect of mental health" (2014, p. 81). Students need to know that their teacher will never ridicule or embarrass them, or let anyone else do so.

If a student senses that the teacher can't keep everybody safe on a psychological and emotional level, her limbic system will immediately go from green to orange, on standby for red.

Here is an example of delivering a safety message: One student says something to another student that sounds racist or like a put-down. I call the first student out for it, but when I do, both students brush it off, saying it's no big deal: "This is just how we talk to each other."

This can be a confusing moment for the teacher. Both students are claiming that the comment didn't negatively affect them, so should the teacher let it slide? In fact, this is a great moment to deliver a safety message not only to these two students, but to every student within earshot of the exchange. I take a hard line. "I don't care if it's said in jest. I don't care if the other person isn't offended. You will not talk to each other this way in my classroom."

The message I am communicating is that I will defend the safety of the learning space by protecting everyone within it from being spoken to that way. If I don't deliver this message, it may be true that neither of the two students involved is hurt by their inappropriate banter, but other students will see that this kind of talk is allowed in my classroom, which lowers the safety for everyone.

The message "You are safe" includes assurance that students are safe *from me* as well, in both words and actions. This means that I do not give myself permission to be temperamental, even when it feels justified. I do not respond sarcastically to a student, even if I think the student deserves it and I know it will get a laugh from the rest of the class. If I ever speak to a student in a way that leaves them embarrassed, I apologize. If what I said to that student was heard by others, I apologize in the presence of all who heard it. I don't use threats, intimidation, or manipulation to try to get students to act the way I want them to. For students to relax and bring their best, they need to know they are safe, not just through my words but also through the way I teach the class.

How we deliver messages can be as important as what messages we give. Here are three tips for effective messaging giving:

*Prioritize the nonverbal.* Although it's easy to focus on the words when delivering a message, words don't play the largest part. Studies show that the majority of human communication is nonverbal. This includes body language and tone of voice, as well as other cues that help a person detect nuance and whether the message is genuine. When messages are most effective, the body language, tone of voice, and other elements of the person delivering the message are aligned, supporting the message's content.

*Timing matters.* With practice, you will start to see ideal moments to deliver a message—moments when you have a *Yes* for delivering that message and the recipient is most open to receiving it. One message delivered to the right person at the right time can be life changing.

*Messages are effective only when delivered individually.* While it's tempting, for the sake of efficiency, to try to deliver a message to a whole class at once, a message delivered to a group is never as impactful as a personal message. People need to feel specifically seen in order to let a positive message in.

While there are other kinds of messages people need to hear, the seven offered in this chapter form a good classroom starter kit. Delivering these messages frequently will give every student in your class the sense that they are appreciated, that they belong, and that they are safe. Experiment with giving the messages, and watch what happens.

**REFLECTION QUESTIONS**

*Grab a notebook and something to write with and respond to the following questions:*

1 When you were in school, what kinds of messages did you receive from teachers?
2 What are some positive messages that you can see yourself giving to students in your classes?
3 For each of these messages, what is a circumstance in which you can see yourself offering it?

# 18

# The Importance of Positive Messages for Teachers

Before I became a teacher, I waited tables at fancy restaurants. I loved being a tipped employee because every tip meant more to me than money; a tip was a message that said, "Good job," or "I appreciate you for what you did." After a busy night of serving customers, I would walk out under the stars with my pockets bulging with cash and my heart full of messages.

Money is one means by which messages are given. A Christmas bonus is a message. But so is a promotion and a corner office. In the private sector, good employers are attuned to the importance of messages when it comes to retaining and supporting valuable employees. Many people assume that it's the money that motivates employees, but the most significant motivator is the messages of being valued, of being appreciated, of being seen for the hard work that are embedded in the money.

In education, the emphasis on making sure that employees feel valued is notably absent. There are no promotions available for teachers, no extra perks to celebrate stand-out performances. In fact, the typical school is a message desert for teachers.

An obvious message source for teachers would be the administrator they work under, but administrators are often so busy that the only time they step into a classroom is to conduct a formal observation. For many teachers, these observations are anxiety producing and not conducive to awakening a teacher's best self.

DOI: 10.4324/9781003360513-21

During the post-observation meeting, the focus is often on the teacher's shortcomings rather than on his strengths. This focus can sideline the seeking system in the teacher's brain and replace it with the fear system, possibly activating a stress reaction as well, and making it difficult for the teacher to hear the feedback as anything other than criticism.

Another possible source for positive messages is other teachers. However, teachers rarely see each other teach. Because teachers don't really know what their colleagues are doing, it is hard for teachers to offer meaningful positive messages to one another.

Students are the only people who observe what teachers do every day. But students don't have the context to truly see and appreciate what is involved, and it really isn't a student's role to be a message source for a teacher. Although teachers cherish those moments when a student thanks them for a lesson or gives them a card with a handwritten message, for a teacher to depend on students to fulfill their message needs invites inappropriate entanglements.

Nevertheless, it's crucial for teachers to receive positive messages regularly. In general, the harder and more soul-wrenching work a person does, the more messages that person needs to be able to continue bringing their best to the work. Teachers perform one of the hardest jobs and definitely need to be amply resourced with positive messages.

If you as a teacher are working in one of these message deserts, check in with yourself. It's probable that you feel unseen, unappreciated, taken for granted, used, perhaps hurt. You may feel like an overdrawn bank account that every day gets more overdrawn. How can you consistently bring your best self without receiving a continual flow of positive messages? You can't.

We can, however, be proactive when it comes to getting the messages we need. There are three basic things to keep in mind when it comes to messages: avoid getting hurt by negative messages, finding ways to get the messages we need, and deepening our receptivity to positive messages so when they do come our way, we actually let them in where they can do us some good. These points deserve elaboration.

1. *Avoid getting hurt by negative messages.*
Just as positive messages can be a boon to a weary psyche, negative messages can hurt. So it's important to do what we can to protect ourselves from their impact. Negative messages are different from constructive feedback. Negative messages—the critical, judgmental, snarky negatives that people throw at each other—cause damage. They can poison our sense of ourselves, corrupt our sense of safety, and wreck our confidence.

Unfortunately, due to the brain's inherent negativity bias, humans are hardwired to take negative messages to heart. Although it's possible to disregard a negative message, most people find it difficult. They might justify giving serious consideration to a negative message by thinking they can learn from criticism, but the psychological cost far outweighs the potential benefit. Negative messages are toxic to self-esteem. They say more about the person delivering the negative message than they do about the recipient.

One way to keep from taking a negative message to heart is to consider the source. What is their intention in sending this negative message? Is it to tear us down? To bolster their ego? Getting honest about the source of the message and deciding if this is someone we would entrust with our self-esteem can break the spell that otherwise lets us allow the message in.

Another strategy to keep a negative message at bay is to imagine it is directed toward someone we love, maybe a spouse or a child. If the message giver had said the same thing to our loved one, would we want our loved one to take that message to heart? If not, that's a cue to love ourselves enough to trash the message.

Some of us are so conditioned to accept negatives that we automatically let them in, not even realizing it until we notice we are upset. A telltale sign that you have taken in a negative message is that you start ruminating on it—playing the message and the situation over and over in your mind. Ruminating on a negative message deepens the damage.

If you notice that you've let in a negative message, you can get your system to release it by taking advantage of the body-mind connection, and performing a physical action that cues the release while associating that action with the release of the message. For instance, you can associate the negative message with a rock and throw the rock into a bush. Or you can associate the negative message with a wad of toilet paper, crumple it up, and flush it down the toilet. You can associate the negative message with something you shouldn't have eaten and then cough, associating the coughs with the idea of coughing up the negative message. Then spit it out.

2.  *Embolden yourself to ask for positive messages.*
    To take care of our message needs, the second thing we need to do is embolden ourselves to ask for positive messages.

    You may have had the experience of putting great effort into something only to have it go unacknowledged. For example, let's say you prepared a presentation to deliver to the staff. After the presentation, your colleagues leave to get ready for their next class. No one says a thing. You try to shrug it off, telling yourself it's fine, people are busy. But deep down, it bothers you; you feel unappreciated.

    Perhaps the next day a colleague says, "Great job on that staff presentation." This is good, and you receive the message graciously, but somehow it doesn't feel like what you need to hear. Then you realize that what you really crave is a message about how hard you worked to make the presentation both interesting and useful. Message needs are often quite specific.

    We can think of positive messages as the equivalent of food for our psychology. They are so important to our well-being and our ability to do our jobs from our best self that when they aren't forthcoming, we need to ask for them. This may mean going to a trusted colleague after that presentation and saying, "Hey, about that presentation I did, I worked hard to make it both interesting and useful. I would love to hear how you experienced that."

People are naturally reluctant to ask for messages. It makes us vulnerable. We may feel like asking reveals a weakness. It puts us at other people's mercy. It can feel like we are being egoic. I understand this and also experience this reluctance, but when I realize that what's at stake is literally my ability to contribute my best, it becomes easier to set aside my reticence and, in spite of the discomfort, ask for a message.

One reason we might not want to ask for a message is fear that if the person responds dismissively, we can end up hurt. We can minimize this risk by selecting people whom we trust and then asking them for a message at a time and place that allows them to pause and actually pay attention to us.

If the members of your PLC are open to the idea, build a round of messages into each meeting—set aside a few minutes at the start for people to give and receive messages. The message prompt can be as simple as what you admire or appreciate about each other. You can also invite members to ask for a particular message they need. Building positive messages into your meeting routine will allow everyone to benefit without the risk of hurt feelings.

To be psychologically healthy and to bring our best to our jobs, receiving positive messages is not optional; they provide the boost that can determine whether we thrive at this job or end up shattered by it.

3. *Learn to let in positive messages.*
Finally, for messages to do their work of boosting our psychological health, we need to let positive messages in when they are available. Whenever a message, whether positive or negative, is directed to us, it's up to us to either receive it or deflect it away. It is not uncommon for people to dismiss a positive message, even when they are in dire need of a message.

One reason people deflect positive messages is that the message feels contrary to how they see themselves. If, for instance, deep down a person feels unlovable (usually due to past negative messages they've received or how they've interpreted past experiences), it may be hard for that person to receive a message of love and acceptance. Paradoxically, that message is exactly the one the person needs to let in to build a healthier sense of himself.

An approach I use to help myself let in a positive message is to say, "Thank you. I'll let that in." Then with the next inhalation, let myself breathe in the message. This practice both honors the person who has made the effort to deliver the message and cues my system to be receptive.

We need an educational culture in which the human need for positive messages is honored, and giving, and asking for, messages is normalized as common practice. Positive messages activate the best self of everyone—teachers, administrators, support staff, and students alike. None of us are self-sufficient when it comes to messages; we need each other to call up our best. To remain in education and stay psychologically healthy, positive messages aren't optional. We need them. Our colleagues need to hear them. Freely giving and receiving positive messages brings us closer to turning schools into the supportive communities of learning they are meant to be.

 **REFLECTION QUESTIONS**

*Grab a notebook and something to write with and respond to the following questions:*

1  How often do you receive positive messages for the work you do and what you bring to your job as an educator?
2  What do you notice about yourself when it comes to letting in positive messages?
3  What is one action you can take today to help yourself receive the messages that you need to be at your best?

# Part III

## Tools for Emotionally Challenging Moments

# 19

# Intervening in the Steps from Dr. Jekyll to Mr. Hyde

According to a 2022 Rand Corporation research report, teachers experience frequent job-related stress at twice the rate of other working adults, making them particularly susceptible to stress reactions while on the job. To be effective, teachers need a greater-than-average capacity to manage the high-stress, volatile circumstances they will encounter in the classroom. Some members of other high-stress professions, such as soldiers and police officers, receive training in regulating stress reactions. Lacking such training, it's simply by the grace of good intentions that teachers do as well as they do.

In Part II of this book, we explored approaches to teaching that would help us teach from our best self and inspire our students to interact with us from theirs. When applied, each of the approaches offer high ROI, setting the stage for many rewarding days in the classroom. Yet there will still be days when events overwhelm us and our ability to remain in our best self falters.

Caught in the throes of a stress reaction, a teacher stands before her students without full access to her neocortex, shot through with adrenaline, trembling, and dry mouthed. Or even worse, along with prompting that stress reaction, the circumstances awaken an unresolved trauma, and the dark hand of a

DOI: 10.4324/9781003360513-23

hurtspot drags her into an underworld of a secret pain. Suddenly, the lovable teacher transforms into a version of Ms. Hyde.

Events that topple us from our best self can come from a myriad of unexpected directions. Maybe a student arrives already triggered and blows up in our classroom, inciting a contagion of stress and hurtspot reactions throughout the class and setting us off in the process. Maybe we receive an email that makes our heart drop to the pit of our stomach just as students are surging into the room. Or maybe, after an already stressful day, one student says or does the thing that fries our last nerve.

Whether we have tools for moments like these can make the difference between whether we remain in the profession for decades, positively impacting thousands of young people, or find the profession unendurable and leave.

In fact, we can train ourselves to interrupt both stress and hurtspot reactions once they get started. Although we may feel as helpless as Dr. Jekyll as he transforms into Mr. Hyde, all of us have stopped a stress reaction before it got the better of us. We do this every time we are startled by a jump scare in a darkened theater or, in my case, when my wife good-naturedly jumps out from behind a corner to scare me.

If she is successful in startling me, my nervous system fires, and I feel a jolt of adrenaline as I jerk away from the blurred figure leaping at me from the shadows. In that moment, a stress reaction initiates in my brain. My limbic system has cocked the hammer, and I am a heartbeat away from freezing, fighting, or fleeing. But rather than throw punches or run out of the house, as soon as I recognize my wife, who is now doubled over laughing at me, I abort the stress reaction and laugh along with her. Not only is it possible for me to avert a stress reaction, once one gets started, my wife counts on it. We all have this ability. The creators of horror films and the makers of haunted houses trust our innate capacity to suspend stress reactions before they get the better of us.

The fact that an initiated stress reaction can be interrupted means that we can learn to consciously avert them even after they've been set in motion. Although hurtspot reactions may be more difficult to turn aside than stress reactions, we can learn

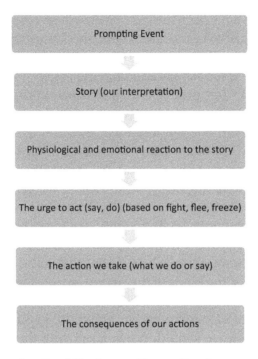

**FIGURE 19.1** Steps from Best Self to Stress or Hurtspot Reaction

Source: Adapted from Aguilar (2018, p. 47)

to bring awareness to the process that triggers them and avoid acting on the thoughts and feelings that an activated hurtspot dredges up.

When a stress or hurtspot reaction fires in us, we experience it instantaneously, as if someone pulled a switch. However, the activation actually involves a series of subconscious steps. Once these steps are made conscious, we can learn to intervene in the process before it takes us around the bend.

The following are the six steps a person takes on the ride from their best self all the way to a full-blown stress or hurtspot reaction:

1. *The prompting event.*
   Every stress reaction begins with a prompting event, which could be anything a person's limbic system registers as a threat. In the case of our prehistoric ancestors,

it may have been the sudden arrival of a predator in camp or a fight over resources with another group.

For modern humans, the prompting events typically look less heroic. We feel our connection with our hunter-gatherer forbears when we sit down to pay our bills and realize that an unexpected expense has left us short for the month. We tap into their ancestral gift as we swerve to avoid another driver veering into our lane. We know something of their emotional lives when, in the aftermath of an argument with a lover, we lie awake in bed, body trembling, heart racing, hurtful thoughts churning through our brain like clothes in a washing machine.

Though the prompting event initiates the same processes in our minds and bodies that it did for Stone-Age humans, the kinds of threats we are most likely to face are threats to our social standing, our financial security, our sense of belonging, or our ability to do our jobs the way we think we should. When faced with threats like these, running away, fighting, or freezing in place are impractical solutions, so in the throes of a stress reaction, we may attempt to repress our instinctual urge and internalize the stress. Over time, this erodes our physical and mental health like corrosive acid.

2. *The story we tell ourselves (our interpretation).*
When faced with a prompting event, our brain makes an instinctual assessment of whether the event is an actual threat or something akin to my wife jumping out from behind the breakfast bar. To make this assessment, the brain pulls upon its vast powers of story-making.

In this context, I'm using "story" to mean the interpretation we bring to a person, situation, or event. In other words, a story is the meaning we create about an experience. The human brain is hardwired to give meaning to experience. From the clay of raw experience, faster than the speed of light, our brain invents stories, complete with heroes, villains, and conflicts charged with drama.

We are so steeped in story that we barely recognize the fact that it drives everything we do, everything we think we know. We plot, we strategize, we gossip, we try to gain advantage, we pit ourselves against antagonists, we strive to conquer, to triumph. Our interpretations of what is happening arise in our minds automatically, and when they do, we tend to believe them.

For most people, the first thing that comes to mind when they hear the word "story" is something untrue, but this isn't always the case. In fact, stories (and the maps we make from them) are most useful when they are informed by knowledge. Through hundreds of generations of experimentation, failure, struggle, and success, human beings have, at great cost, slowly built a storehouse of knowledge that we use to tell stories that are increasingly harmonious with reality. These stories about how things work allow us to build airplanes that fly and rocket ships that travel to the moon. We consider such stories "true" because we use them to make accurate maps that help us move, create, build, and thrive in our environment. The more we allow knowledge to influence our stories, the truer our stories become, and the more successful we are.

I can avert a stress reaction when my wife jumps out from behind the counter because my brain is able to draw upon prior knowledge to create a true story. As she leaps toward me, my brain automatically reaches for a story to make sense of what is happening. It assigns her a role as a character, be it friend, threat, or neutral figure. As soon as my brain registers her as my loving but mischievous wife, the story of potential threat is displaced by the true story that I am not under threat, and the stress reaction process stops. Had my story making brain assigned her the role of a threat, the stress reaction process would have proceeded, leading to a very different outcome.

When faced with a prompting event, the stories that naturally spring up are rarely true stories. Rather, they are generated in the super-computer of our subconscious, which leans toward interpreting events through its built-in negativity bias. Using data from past experiences, familial influences, hurtspots, cultural messages, available knowledge, and other believed stories, our subconscious is likely to generate not a true story, but a story that might have helped our prehistoric ancestors survive but that doesn't offer us much advantage today. In the typical hurly-burly of day-to-day teaching, it is easy for our brains to come up with stories that needlessly hurl us into stress and hurtspot reactions.

For example, what stories spring to your mind in the following three prompting events?

1. For the third time today, just as you are finally getting the class focused on the lesson, an announcement is made over the intercom.
2. Rather than doing the assignment, Emily is sitting back in her chair, arms folded, with a scowl on her face.
3. Julian repeatedly talks to his friend during your instruction, and when you ask him to move to another seat in the room, he ignores you.

If you are like most people, the stories that came to mind cast someone else—the person speaking over the intercom, Emily, Julian—as the villain undermining your ability to do your job. Although it made sense for our prehistoric ancestors that the worst, most cynical interpretation was the first to pop up on the limbic system's search engine of assumptions, in complex modern society, and particularly in our classrooms, believing that first-arising story is likely to trigger a stress reaction that prompts us to take action that may do more harm than good.

3. *Our physiological and emotional reaction to the story.*
When the story-maker in us interprets a situation as threatening, the limbic system immediately initiates a stress or hurtspot reaction, flooding us with negative feelings, judgments, and uncomfortable physical sensations just as it did in our Paleolithic ancestors. We naturally assume that the arising thoughts, feelings, and sensations are directly caused by the prompting event, but this is not the case. Our physiological and emotional reaction is caused by our interpretation of the prompting event—in other words, our story.

For instance, if the story I tell myself about Julian is that he is intentionally disrespecting me in order to embarrass me in front of the class, my limbic system will register him as a threat. This sets off a chain of chemical reactions that disengages my neocortex while strengthening the dominance of my mammalian and reptilian brains. My body is flooded with adrenaline in the same way adrenaline flooded my prehistoric ancestor's body when he saw a member of another tribe stealing his food.

4. *The urge to act (say, do—based on fight, flee, or freeze).*
   Once the physiological and emotion reaction takes place, we are primed for action. The urge to say or do something right now feels overwhelming, and we feel compelled to act or react, based on our story. This is when I decide to give Julian a piece of my mind.

5. *What I do or say.*
   What I do or say is the next step. I may raise my voice. I may criticize Julian for being disrespectful.

6. *The consequences.*
   The final step of this six-step process is the aftermath. What is my state of being as I proceed through the rest of my day? How does Julian feel about my class and the lesson now? How safe is the learning environment in my classroom? All of these factors directly depend on whether or not I interrupted the stress reaction process or let it take over.

Let's see how these steps work in a road rage scenario in order to identify where best to intervene in the stress reaction sequence before it gets the better of us. Here's an interesting fact: an AAA Foundation study of more than 10,000 road rage incidents found that they resulted in at least 218 murders and another 12,610 injuries (*Road Rage*, 2013).

When someone cuts us off on the freeway, our brain immediately generates a story that casts the other driver as a villain and us the protagonist of a story. Judgments and insults about this villainous driver arise in our head. A stress and possibly hurtspot reaction is initiated. Our system is flooded with negative emotions about this person who has so callously threatened our life. Without knowing this person, we already hate him.

Our reptilian brain compels us to fight this scoundrel. We lean on our horn, tailgate, or maybe flip him the bird. In a split second, we have traveled through all six steps in the sequence from our best self to our own version of Mr. Hyde, taken over by a stress reaction.

But our actions are not taken in a vacuum. Whatever action we take can easily become a prompting event for the other driver. He hears us honking, sees us flip him off, and then makes up a story about us in which he is the good guy and we are the asshole. He experiences his own physiological and emotional reaction to his story of being accosted by an asshole driver. These sensations and emotions compel him to act, so he slams on his brakes and yells at us out his window.

Now his actions become a further prompting event for us, driving us deeper into our stress or hurtspot reaction.

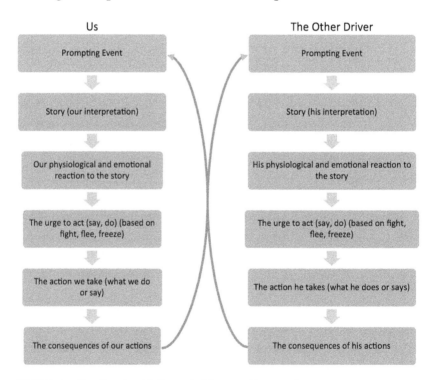

**FIGURE 19.2** Two People with Entangled Stress or Hurtspot Reactions

Every escalating action one of us takes becomes a prompting event for the other to escalate the confrontation further. Taken to extreme, this becomes a dance of death, as each party mindlessly performs the steps of a pre-choreographed dance until one person is dead and the other is in prison. Fortunately, in most road rage cases, it doesn't go that far. One of us turns off the freeway or accelerates away. But even if the worst is averted, we are still left with that lousy feeling of having been wronged—the sick feeling in our gut, the dry mouth, the anxiety, the seething emotions and roiling thoughts. We are so far from our best self that it could ruin the rest of our day, and it could easily pollute how we relate to our family when we return home.

At what point in this terrible process can we intervene and create a different result? AAA and other agencies who offer advice about road rage focus on step 5, the action step, making recommendations such as "don't use aggressive gestures, don't honk, don't tailgate, don't pull off to the side of the road to settle this 'man to man'" (*Road Rage*, 2013). But by step 5, we are already trapped in a full-blown stress reaction. Intervening at the action step means we have to suppress the urge to fight, which costs us energy, leaving us stewing in judgments and negative emotions. To retain our best self, the process needs to be interrupted at an earlier step, before Mr. Hyde takes the wheel.

Let's see where we might intervene in the process earlier, before we've lost ourselves. The prompting event is the same—some guy in an SUV cuts us off. The word "asshole" immediately arises from the darkness of our subconscious. We see the story that flows from that—he is the monster who just threatened our life. But instead of mindlessly believing that story, we question the story with a single word: *maybe*.

*Maybe* he is an asshole. On the other hand, *maybe* he's in a hurry to get somewhere—*maybe* to a job interview or his daughter's music recital. Any number of things could be the reason he is distracted and not paying attention. The truth is, *we don't know*. We don't have the knowledge needed to act with justification on the story that just materialized in our head. In fact, when we think about it, *we've all made errors while driving, probably even inadvertently cutting people off. One thing we can be sure of, it isn't*

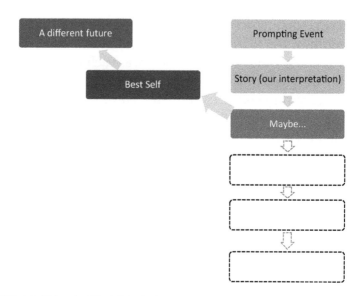

**FIGURE 19.3** Using the Word "Maybe" to Interrupt a Stress Reaction

*personal. To him, we're just another car on the road.* Then, we forget about him, turn up our music, and drive on relaxed and content.

What I'm recommending is the same thing we teach our students: don't act on opinions, do your research, use credible sources, make sure you can back up your claims with evidence. When I question the story that arises in my head about the other driver, I am using the principle of *uke*. I receive the arising story with the word *"maybe,"* as in *"maybe* he is an asshole." And then I redirect the story with the word *but*, because the truth is, *"I don't really know."*

By questioning the arising story, I am able to continue on with my drive from my best self. Inserting *maybe* at the story-making step essentially puts me in the same position I'm in when, after being startled by my wife, I recognize her laughing at me and realize that I'm not under an actual threat. In that moment I displace the story that would have otherwise led me through the sequence of a stress reaction.

When a student disrespects you in the classroom—when he is willfully defiant, derails your class with an absurd or disruptive remark, challenges you, criticizes the lesson, or ignores you entirely—remember the power of *maybe* to question the story that appears in your head about this student. Then redirect it with *but I don't really know*. The truth is, we lack the knowledge to elevate our story to the status of a true story from which to map out an effective action plan.

When we lack knowledge, we can resort to being curious. Be curious about the student's home life, about what happened last night or this morning, about whether he's eaten breakfast, about his need for attention. Curiosity frees us from the confines of a limiting story so we can be present in the grand palace of *I don't know but I can learn*.

Ask the student to step outside. Join him when you get the rest of the class settled and say something like: "I noticed that when I asked you to move to another seat, you ignored me. Help me understand why you didn't do as I asked." Then listen to what he has to say. From this conversation, a story will emerge (one always does), and this story will be informed by knowledge. After listening, respond to the situation as appropriate from your best self, and then get back to teaching.

 **REFLECTION QUESTIONS**

*Grab a notebook and something to write with and respond to the following questions:*

1   Think of a stress or hurtspot reaction you've had recently (either in or outside the classroom). Reflect on what you experienced during each step of the process.
    a.  *The prompting event*
    b.  *Your story*
    c.  *Your physical and emotional response to the story*
    d.  *The action you felt impelled to take*
    e.  *The action you took*
    f.  *The consequences*
2   How could a change in the story have shifted this process?

# 20

# The Cool Pause

As we saw in the road rage example in Chapter 19, reactive human beings do and say things that become prompting events for other human beings. When this happens in the classroom, teachers get caught in power struggles.

Let's say you're up in front teaching the class when you notice Erin sneakily scrolling through her phone. You've already reminded her twice in the last 15 minutes to put her phone away. It's near the end of the day, and you've had enough. In your head, a story arises, seemingly of its own accord: *This is flagrant disrespect.*

Your limbic system registers a threat to your authority as the teacher, and now you're hurtling down the tracks of a stress reaction. Your heart rate increases, and your cheeks start to burn. You feel compelled to act. You raise your voice. "Erin, I've told you twice already to put your phone away. Now you've lost it for the period. Give it to me," and you extend a trembling hand.

Your action becomes a prompting event for Erin. A story arises in her brain in which you are the villain who is trying to bully her into giving up her phone. Her limbic system throws her into a stress reaction. Her heart rate increases, her muscles tense. She feels the urge to defy you, to insult you. Your stress reaction process and Erin's are now entangled.

What happens next can be boiled down to two possibilities. The first is that Erin hands over her phone. If she does, she is

DOI: 10.4324/9781003360513-24

likely to do so resentfully, with a passive-aggressive display of attitude. Then she will sit in her seat stewing, miles away from the lesson, ruminating on how unfair this is. Her mind will come up with examples of other students who had their phones out during class with zero consequences.

The second possibility is that Erin will escalate, defying your command. "Hell no, I'm not giving you my phone." Her defiance now becomes a second prompting event for you, which drives you deeper into your stress reaction, and you feel compelled to say or do something that escalates the conflict. This, in turn, feeds her reactive state. Both of you are now throwing gasoline on each other's stress reactions and spiraling into worst-self hell.

Power struggles like these turn the Best Self Model of Teaching and Learning upside down, with teachers and students bringing out the worst in each other and trashing the learning environment in the process.

When faced with a prompting event, as soon as we notice the arising story, what we need is a beat of time. We need at least the space of a breath to gather ourself and to wedge the word *"maybe"* into the arising story.

After inserting *maybe*, we could take a second breath and apply one of the other approaches in this book. We could receive the situation from *uke* and find our *Yes*. We could remember our Prime Directive. We could remember radical acceptance.

How much time do we need? Not much. The span of a few heartbeats is enough to interrupt the stress reaction process and reestablish our best self.

When it came to having a reason to take this beat of time, our grandparents' generation had an advantage. From the 1940s through the 1960s, almost half of American adults smoked. As we now know, the health repercussions were horrendous and included lung cancer, heart disease, and a shortened life span. However, for creating the necessary interval of time to avert a stress reaction, smoking was perfect.

In the face of a prompting event, a smoker had a socially sanctioned reason to pause. She could pull a cigarette from its package, light it, inhale, and blow out the smoke before responding. This allowed her to assert control over the timing of her response. Recent research on animals indicates that having a sense of control may be the deciding factor in whether a person keeps their cool or falls apart under stress (Arnsten et al., 2021).

A second advantage smoking offered was that it looked cool. Over the decades, filmmakers have capitalized on the cache of cool that an actor smoking a cigarette can bring to a scene. Looking cool, or at least attempting to look cool, is more beneficial than it seems. To put attention on looking cool recalibrates the limbic system's assessment of the situation because, unless we're James Bond, if we're bothering to look cool, we're likely not facing an actual threat to life and limb.

When Erin pulls out that phone, you need a cool pause—just enough time to take a drag from a cigarette and coolly exhale the smoke before responding. For good reasons, teachers aren't allowed to smoke in their classrooms, but when faced with a prompting event, a teacher can take other actions that give her the time she needs. She can adjust an article of clothing, take a leisurely sip of a drink, make a note on a notepad, run her fingers through her hair, bring the tip of a pen to her lips.

Whether we succeed in looking cool is less important than taking the time needed to opt out of the stress reaction and engage the situation from our best self.

The cool pause gives us the space to respond rather than react. Our response creates a different future from the one that would have derived from our stress or hurtspot reaction. In this new outcome, the student is better off, and so are we.

The trick is remembering to take that cool pause, and for that there is a learning curve. In the aftermath of a stressful situation, you might find yourself thinking: *I could have used a cool pause there*. Remembering the cool pause after a stressful exchange is progress—one step closer to remembering it during the exchange. Be patient with yourself and experiment. Before you know it, you'll be the unflappable teacher who uses cool pauses so well that situations rarely get the better of you.

**REFLECTION QUESTIONS**

*Grab a notebook and something to write with and respond to the following questions:*

1   Make a list of prompting events that tend to trigger in you a stress or hurtspot reaction.
2   Make a list of props within reach in your classroom that you could use to create a cool pause.
3   For each prop, what might you do with it to make it look cool?

# 21

# The Importance of Giving Triggered Students Space

From the spaciousness achieved with a cool pause, a teacher may notice that one of her students is caught up in their own stress or hurtspot reaction. The student might have entered the classroom that way, or they might have been set off by another student or by something the teacher did or said. Whatever the prompting event, the subsequent process into a stress or hurtspot reaction was purely mechanical. The fact that the student is triggered is not worth taking personally.

As we have seen, a stress reaction typically takes one of three forms. A student experiencing a "fight" response may be gruff or curt. When pushed, they may become belligerent, aggressive, or insulting toward the teacher or another student in the classroom. A student experiencing a freeze reaction may become quiet and attempt to disappear. They may seem on the brink of tears. Fleeing, the third option, may look like retreating inside their hoodie. However the stress reaction manifests, the student no longer has access to their higher brain function. Trying to get a student to demonstrate an academic skill while in this state is folly that will only deepen their reactivity.

Sometimes the wisest teaching move is to let a triggered student be. When I notice that a student is upset, particularly withdrawn, or seemingly angry, I try to set up conditions that make it easy for him to return to his best self so he can learn.

DOI: 10.4324/9781003360513-25

If I am confident in my relationship with him, I may privately say, "I don't know, but it looks to me like this might be a hard day for you. Is that true?" Typically, the student will nod. "Got it. I'm sorry about that. I appreciate that you came to class even though you're having a hard day. Let me know what I can do to support you, okay?"

And that's it. Saying or doing more would only complicate things. Then I keep an eye on him. If he shows signs of being ready to participate, I encourage it, but I don't push.

In many schools, teachers are expected to keep every student engaged during every minute of every class, but this expectation isn't based in reality. The prerequisite for learning is an open, relaxed state of being in which the learner can access his whole brain. A student caught in a stress or hurtspot reaction has lost this access. His limbic system is diverting his body's learning resources to the pressing job of saving his life. He might as well be caught in a burning building, panicky to find a way out. In such a situation, math isn't a priority. Trying to force him to engage in the lesson will lead him to see you as an additional threat, compounding his struggle and prompting him to say and do things that will force your hand, likely provoking you to lose your best self, jeopardizing the learning environment, and leading to discipline consequences for him.

We can avoid all of this by simply giving the triggered student space and a message that he is safe and supported, granting him the room he needs to return to his best self while keeping the learning partnership with him intact.

 **REFLECTION QUESTIONS**

*Grab a notebook and something to write with and respond to the following questions:*

1 Put yourself in the seat of a triggered student in your class. If you were that student, what would you want from your teacher?

2 What could a teacher do or say that would help you, as that student, find your way back to your best self?

# 22

# Speaking the Language of the Limbic System

The principles and approaches offered in this book so far can help us retain that whole-brain, internally aligned, best version of ourself. Yet there will still be conditions and situations that will push us beyond our capacity. Sometimes we're going to lose it.

Wouldn't it be great if at the moment we notice ourselves slipping into a stress or hurtspot reaction, we could dial up our limbic system? We could give it a heads-up, letting it know we're not in actual physical danger and there's no need to set in motion the physiological processes designed to save our life. Although we have no such direct hotline, we do have two indirect avenues through which we can communicate with our limbic system: breath and vision.

Both breath and vision, along with heart rate, digestion, sexual arousal, and blood pressure, are under the control of our autonomic nervous system. This is the system that controls all the functions of the body that we don't have to think about, freeing us to go through our days without having to make our heart beat or tell our kidneys to filter blood.

Among all the functions that the autonomic nervous system governs, only breathing and vision can also be consciously controlled. We can go years, if we want, just letting breathing do its thing, and the inhaling and exhaling will reliably go on without our giving it a single thought. However, we can also hold

DOI: 10.4324/9781003360513-26

our breath. We can slow it down and speed it up. We can make ourselves breathe more deeply or more shallowly. Likewise, we can keep vision functions on automatic, or we can assert manual control and either narrow or expand our field of view.

The autonomic nervous system basically has two parts: the parasympathetic nervous system and the sympathetic nervous system. The parasympathetic nervous system is in charge during nonthreatening conditions, quietly overseeing the processes of digesting food, fighting off disease, and giving us access to our whole brain so we can come up with novel ideas for running our classroom. When the limbic system hits the stress alarm, the sympathetic nervous system takes over, diverting all the available physiological resources away from these functions to your muscles so you can save your life.

As teachers, if we had that hotline to our limbic system, we could let it know that Anthony's use of choice language to express his opinion about an assignment is not a threat to our life, and ask it to please return us to our parasympathetic nervous system. Lacking this hotline, we can communicate with our limbic system through the channels of breath and vision.

Let's first look at breath. When the limbic system senses a threat and cues the sympathetic nervous system to take over, among the host of changes that occur in the body is a shift to rapid breathing, often high in the chest. The limbic system is particularly attuned to our breathing pattern. Rapid breathing tells the limbic system that our life is still in the process of being saved, which reinforces the engagement of the sympathetic nervous system. Conversely, when the breath is deep and calm, the limbic system concludes that the threat has passed. The parasympathetic nervous system is called back to its post, and convivial Dr. Jekyll returns.

We can use this signaling between the breath and the limbic system to our advantage. By intentionally taking slow, deep breaths, we can give our limbic system a heads-up to break off the stress reaction and return us to our best self.

One extremely effective technique, used by Navy SEALS and first responders, is box breathing. There are four steps to box breathing, just as there are four sides to a box. Prior to initiating box breathing, the person releases all the air from their lungs. Then they

1. Slowly inhale to a count of four
2. Hold that breath for a count of four
3. Exhale to a count of four
4. Hold the exhale for a count of four

In these basic directions, each side of the box is four counts. However, depending on the person's lung capacity, the box can be made smaller or larger—for instance, giving each side of the box three counts for those with less lung capacity and five counts for those with more. Regardless of the number, the counts should be slow and steady. The four-step process is repeated until the person feels their shoulders relax, tension release from their hands and face, and their best self return.

Box breathing can be a particularly powerful inoculant against a stress reaction when done prior to entering a stressful situation. In fact, the Navy SEALS use box breathing to steel themselves before a mission. Given that one of the United States' most elite fighting forces trusts box breathing before sending SEALS into firefights, a few preparatory box breaths are likely to help you retain your best self during that meeting with an angry parent.

Another useful breath technique is the physiological sigh. One advantage to this technique is that it is easy to conceal. It's also extremely effective. According to Dr. Andrew Huberman, a neuroscientist at Stanford University, the physiological sigh is the fastest way to bring a stressed body back to baseline (2021, p. 61). The person takes two inhalations through the nose, followed by an extended exhalation through the mouth. Typically, the first inhale through the nose is longer than the second, followed by a long, releasing exhale. That's it. In the classroom, a physiological sigh can be disguised as a case of the sniffles. One to three physiological sighs are typically enough to bring a person out of a stress-reactive state and back to their best self.

The second autonomic process that bridges the unconscious and the conscious is vision. Under stress, our pupils dilate, our field of view narrows, and our eyeballs rotate to a set depth of field on a single point. This allows us to see the source of the threat with acute clarity while the surroundings become blurry. This visual zeroing in on a perceived threat activates the sympathetic nervous system, flooding our body with the needed neurotransmitters and hormones to save our life. We feel agitated, ready to fight, flee, or freeze (Huberman, 2021, pp. 60–61). The person we are focusing on this way now perceives us as a threat, and the power struggle ensues.

In contrast, when we are in a relaxed state, our vision tends to naturally adopt a wide, panoramic view. This is the same mode of viewing we use when watching a sunset—an expansive view that includes great depth.

As with the breath, we can use this physiological link between vision and the limbic system to our advantage. We can efficiently shift out of a stress reaction by intentionally adopting a wide-angle, soft-eyes style of vision. Once we have a panoramic view, we can enhance the communication to our limbic system by broadening our awareness to include other senses, taking in ambient sounds and smells and physical sensations. Widening our field of vision while consciously hearing the furnace or air conditioner blowing in the classroom and feeling our feet on the floor sends an all-clear message to the limbic system—there is no threat. It can return us to our parasympathetic nervous system and our best self.

**REFLECTION QUESTIONS**

*Grab a notebook and something to write with and respond to the following questions:*

1 For 30 seconds, intentionally breathe high in your chest and extremely rapidly while focusing your awareness on a disturbing thought or memory. Write a description of the thoughts and feelings that arise.
2 Now do three box breaths and two physiological sighs while using panoramic vision that is both wide angle and has a depth of field. Write a description of the thoughts and feelings that arise.

# 23

# Using Counter-Stories to Recover from Hurtspot Reactions

Although breath and vision techniques work well for recovering from stress reactions, climbing out of a hurtspot reaction often takes a bit more. Besides throwing us into stress reactivity and flooding us with distressing emotions, hurtspot reactions cause us to experience ourselves through a damaging story. To escape the grip of a hurtspot reaction as quickly as possible, we need to bring a counter-story to the story that the hurtspot has awakened within us.

When we are children, our childmind does its best to make sense of difficult, sometimes even traumatic, situations. It uses story to interpret and give meaning to those experiences. The stories we create about ourselves under the pressure of trauma are invariably negative ones, such as *I am bad* or *No matter what I do, it's never enough.* These stories become shorthand interpretations about ourselves and the world. In the misty realm of our subconscious, we carry those stories into adulthood, along with the childhood pain that remains locked up with the story. These become hurtspots that topple us from our best self whenever an experience reminds us of the story we created from the original trauma.

A hurtspot story inclines us to interpret events in particular ways. For instance, during a post-evaluation meeting, the principal might say: "I saw seven students who were not engaged in

DOI: 10.4324/9781003360513-27

the lesson." One teacher might say to himself: *Oh good, feedback. Now I know I need to work on keeping an active field of attention so I can register how engaged all my students are.* Hearing the same feedback, another teacher might think: *My god, what does this guy expect? I'm already at a full run all day every day, and now he dings me because a few resistant students checked out during class. What does it take to ever be enough around here?* The way we react to situations is very much determined by the old stories we carry about ourselves and the world.

Our stories spring into action to help us interpret current situations. For someone with a hurtspot story about *never being good enough*, the administrator's mention of the seven disengaged students could easily throw him into a hurtspot reaction. Once in a reactive state, he would feel compelled to blame the administrator—or blame himself for being such a lousy teacher. If he blames himself, an array of harmful thoughts about himself will spring up in his head: *Oh no, I knew I wasn't cut out for this job. Seven students not engaged … why can't I ever get this right?*

Once we fall into a hurtspot reaction, finding our way out can be challenging. One morning as I was getting ready for classes, the office manager came into my classroom and unloaded on me about something I had said to another staff member. I was the leadership advisor at the time, and a situation had arisen about some leadership money that I didn't understand. I had wondered out loud, in the presence of a colleague, whether this office manager might have made a mistake. God knows I've made my share of mistakes, and I thought she might have made one. Word got back to her. Apparently, her arising story was that I had accused her of being incompetent. This left her feeling completely justified in coming into my classroom before school that morning to read me the riot act. From the pain of a hurtspot, people say and do things in proportion to how they feel, not in proportion to what actually happened. In this case, the woman didn't hold back.

The hurtspot reaction occurring in her prompted her to take an action that precipitated a hurtspot reaction in me. Some people have hurtspots that, when active, make them feel like exploding on someone else. Others have hurtspots that, when active, make them feel like imploding on themselves. Some have both. I have the sort that usually compel me to implode on myself. While the office manager upbraided me, I sat there dumbly taking it while the bombs went off in my body.

My activated hurtspot dropped me into an underworld of pain. For the rest of the day, I was a tangle of anger, hurt, shame, and despair. I felt sick. That night I was kept awake by dark thoughts looping in my head.

This particular set of thoughts and feelings wasn't new to me; I'd had the same miserable reaction dozens of times before—each time set off by a prompting event in which I felt judged or criticized. This got me wondering. Why would I be so devastated by someone else's judgments? Why did I care?

I knew it was possible to be unaffected by criticism. I'd had experiences of someone yelling at me that affected me no more than the sound of a jackhammer—just dumb noise. The week before, a homeless man had unleashed a tirade of curses in my direction. As soon as I understood that I wasn't in danger and the man was not in his right mind, I simply felt sad for him. It didn't ruin my day. So what was different about this situation?

Among the mix of negative thoughts, some about the office manager and some about myself, the ones about myself were especially hard. A deep part of myself was seeing me through her critical eyes and believing that her judgments of me were true.

When the office manager criticized me, she awakened a story I had spent a lifetime trying to repress—a story about being fundamentally flawed that came with a hunk of unprocessed pain. In my weird childmind logic, the fact that she had criticized me confirmed that hurtful story.

Though I wanted to blame her for how miserable I felt, I knew that her storming into my room to give me a piece of her mind wasn't really the problem. The problem was that I had a hurtspot that made me vulnerable to being emotionally destroyed by another person's behavior.

To escape the hurtspot tailspin, I needed to see the current situation through the lens of a counter-story—a new story about the situation that could supplant the hurtspot story that had kidnapped me from my best self. To find my way out of my hurtspot reaction into the light of a better story, I reflected on two questions: *Did I do my best?* and *What can I learn from this experience?*

1.  *Did I do my best?*
    Asking ourselves if we've done our best is a powerful antidote to hurtspot stories, which generally take the form of negative judgments about ourselves. Being able to affirm that *yes, I did my best* is powerful, because our best in any situation is always the best we can do. Logic dictates that our best is enough.

    In this case, my honest answer to this question was *Yes, I did my best.* My best in this situation certainly left room for improvement, but I had nonetheless brought the best I had. Saying this to myself went a long way toward quieting the critical baying hounds in my head.

    Even if I couldn't answer that I had done my best, the second question would still have helped put the hurtspot reaction to rest.

2.  *What can I learn from this experience?*
    We can learn from any experience. Maybe we made a mistake, but who doesn't? In fact, along with our opposable thumbs and a knack for stories, mistake-making may be in the top three of humanity's defining features. So if I made a mistake, fine; I'm human. When I ask myself *What can I learn from this experience?* I am using reflection to turn the experience into an opportunity to grow, to learn, to rise above who I currently am and become someone better.

    In the situation with the office manager, hell yes, there were things I could learn. I could learn to keep my idle musings to myself around some colleagues. I could learn a better system for keeping records so I wouldn't have to rely on an office manager. I could learn that I didn't have to take someone else's unhinged reaction to heart. Most important, I could learn about myself—this hurtspot and how to use reflective questions to create a counter-story to free myself of a hurtspot reaction. To learn from a difficult situation, to transform a blunder into blessings, grants an advantage I can benefit from for the rest of my life. My new counter-story was that I could use my experience with the office manager to improve my ability to use a counter-story to calm a hurtspot reaction, making a better, stronger me in the process. I also learned that I didn't need to take that kind of abuse at work, and in the future, could stop her or walk away.

It's the stories we hold about ourselves that cut us, reduce us, kick us out of the castles of our best self—not what other people say and do. Using those two reflective questions to create a counter-story is the most efficient way I know to rescue ourselves from a hurtspot reaction.

To be clear, this approach is a form of best-self first aid. It helps us recover our best self when we've lost it to a hurtspot reaction. It isn't designed to transmute the underlying hurtspot and thereby prevent future hurtspot reactions. Addressing the hurtspot itself entails learning more about the power that stories have over us and how we can change our stories to create a best self that is not so easily messed with. This is what we explore in Part IV.

 **REFLECTION QUESTIONS**

*Grab a notebook and something to write with and respond to the following questions:*

1 Think of a moment when a hurtspot was triggered in you. What is the old story linked to that hurtspot? Once you've identified the old story, insert the word "maybe" in front of it.
2 Thinking about the incident that stirred up that hurtspot story, answer the following two questions:
   a. *Did I do my best?*
   b. *What can I learn from that experience?*
3 Using your responses to those two questions, construct a counter-story about the event that prompted the hurtspot reaction.

# Part IV
## Creating a Resilient Best Self

# 24

# Having a Hand in the Stories That Make Us

Human beings are driven to make sense of things. It isn't enough for us to know that something happened; we want to know why it happened and what it means. Stories are the medium through which we make sense of raw experience and imbue it with meaning. With stories, we interpret our world and decode life's mysteries. Story is the talisman with which we confront the human condition, our frailty, our awareness of death.

The most useful stories we tell are the ones informed by knowledge. Story is the engine that allows us to take knowledge and do something with it. Knowledge-derived stories take us places—they drive human creativity and achievement.

Most of the stories that run our lives, however, aren't informed by knowledge. As children, we are handed stories from culture and family. As adults, we are flooded with input from advertisers and spokespeople for vested interests who wield the power of story to influence us, to make us buy their products, vote for their candidates, think the way they want us to think, do what they want us to do.

There are two important things to know about stories. First, the stories we tell ourselves about ourselves dictate what is possible for us. Second, although these stories are typically submerged in the subconscious, by bringing awareness to the stories

DOI: 10.4324/9781003360513-29

that run our lives, we can begin to change them. We don't have to live cramped lives inside the bounds of the stories that were handed to us or that we created for ourselves as children. We can use the knowledge that comes with our adult awareness to rewrite the stories we tell about ourselves. And when we change our stories, we change our sense of who we are and, with it, our life prospects, our choices, our behavior, what we can successfully do.

Of all the stories we tell ourselves about ourselves, the ones born from trauma reduce us the most. This is because a traumatic experience leaves a child's psyche with few options other than to create a damaging story about herself. For instance, when a child is beaten by a parent, she has to make sense of why this parent, who she looks to for love and protection, would choose to beat her. This puts her story-making machinery in a bind: who should be placed in the villain role? For a child, it is safer to hate herself than to risk her relationship with a parent by hating the parent, so her psyche generates a story that explains why she deserves to be beaten. She carries the summary of this story forward into adulthood, some version of: *I am bad. I'm not enough. There is something wrong with me.* And she buries the emotional and psychological pain associated with the story in a hurtspot that periodically awakens and torments her through the course of her life.

Whatever our childhood experiences may have been and whatever method we use to manage the hurtspots we carry, we do our best to become functional adults. We get a college degree. We want to make a difference, so we become a teacher. We want to believe that any challenging aspects of our childhood are behind us, and we can now live our life unaffected by them. But then, something happens that awakens one of those hurtspots, and we are carried far from our best self.

One afternoon during my second year of teaching, after the students had left for the day, I noticed that a few of them hadn't put their chairs up on the desks. I walked around putting up chairs—and then I saw, scrawled in pencil on the top of a desk, "Schroder Sucks." My heart fell into my gut. My face flushed.

I felt shame, and anger, and humiliation. *I put my heart and soul into this job, why can't these kids see that?* I felt sick. *Was I really that bad? Why didn't they like me?* I wanted to run. I wanted to find a hole and hide. A part of me wanted to quit my job.

I had tumbled into a hurtspot. I felt ashamed for being so impacted by a 14-year-old's scribbles on a desk. I knew that to succeed at teaching, I needed to be less sensitive to whatever my students thought of me, but how? My hurtspots were always waiting, primed to be set off. To thrive as a teacher, I needed to build a best self that was less susceptible to hurtspot reactions. For that, I needed to change the stories that kept the hurtspots intact.

Research shows that the deeply rooted stories we hold about ourselves can be changed. Daphna Oyserman and her colleagues at the University of Michigan wondered if the low graduation rates among African American and Hispanic students might be linked to their concept of their possible selves—in other words, to the story they told themselves about their own prospects for the future. The researchers recognized that society inundates low-income minority youth with stories of low academic achievement, priming them to construct identities that conform to these limiting stories. So they created an intervention program to help these youth develop a new story for themselves—and thus a new possible self they could live into.

In this program, eighth-grade minority youth who went to school in inner city Detroit attended 11 one-hour sessions during which they were given discussion prompts and activities calculated to help them shift their possible-self story. The control group attended their regular home room classes without the discussion prompts and activities. The researchers then tracked both groups for two years, looking at measures such as attendance rate, GPA, and school retention.

The results were dramatic, as the eighth graders in the intervention emerged from the program with increased initiative around school, higher grades, and better attendance. Even two years after those 11 sessions, they were spending significantly more time on homework, were less disruptive in class, and attended school more regularly than the control group. Between eighth and tenth grades, twice as many students in the control group dropped out of school compared to the students who experienced the intervention (Oyserman et al., 2006).

As this study shows, the stories we tell ourselves about ourselves are malleable. When people change their stories, they change their future.

This pivotal discovery that our stories can be changed prompts the question: is there a best story to tell ourselves about ourselves? Research into the mental and emotional state of people who exhibit a high level of resiliency, who are able to bring their best under pressure and bounce back from setbacks, suggests there is. Resilient people tend to maintain a consistent mindset of what researchers characterize as realistic optimism. Realistic optimists believe in their ability to successfully meet whatever life throws their way; even though they may struggle and stumble, ultimately, they are confident that they can overcome adversity and succeed.

Realistic optimism is not a rosy outlook that blithely assumes all is well; rather, it is a gritty yet positive mindset that empowers a person to face challenges head on. When a realistic optimist faces a setback, she interprets it in a way that allows her to pick up the pieces and move forward (Southwick & Charney, 2018, pp. 35–42).

We all have overcome obstacles. When we use that knowledge to inform our stories about ourselves, making stories that highlight the events in which we have persevered and prevailed, we begin to become realistic optimists, living into the story of a possible self who faces hardship with positivity and confidence.

In the next chapter, we'll look at one astonishingly effective approach for revising our stories, specifically, the stories we've created out of traumatic experiences that tend to leave us with hurtspots.

**REFLECTION QUESTIONS**

*Grab a notebook and something to write with and respond to the following questions*:

1   What is one story you notice yourself telling yourself from time to time that has negatively impacted you in your life?
2   Where do you think you might have picked up this story?
3   How has this story impacted you as a teacher?

# 25

# Using Expressive Writing to Revise Hurtspot Stories

With the right approach, we can change the stories that reduce us and limit our lives. One particularly promising method, called Expressive Writing, involves writing about past traumatic experiences in a way that leads to lasting changes. Through Expressive Writing, we can revise the stories that limit us, extricating ourselves from hurtspots and creating a resilient best self in the process.

Researchers began experimenting with Expressive Writing in the 1980s. The first study was simple. Dr. James Pennebaker and his team assembled 50 college students and told them that they would be writing for 15 minutes a day for four consecutive days. What they wrote would be kept confidential, and they would receive no feedback on their writing. They were then randomly divided into two groups: one group would write about an emotional, traumatic experience, and the other group would write about a superficial, nonemotional topic. The participants writing about a traumatic experience were instructed to explore their deepest thoughts and feelings about that experience and were invited to tie that experience to other parts of their life. If a participant did not have a traumatic experience to write about, they were instructed to write about a major conflict or stressor.

Then each participant was taken to a solitary room to write for 15 minutes (in subsequent research, this was expanded to

DOI: 10.4324/9781003360513-30

20 minutes). Although the participants who wrote about a traumatic experience universally reported finding the exercise helpful, the researchers knew that the real tell would be if the subjects showed measurable changes in the weeks and months that followed. With permission, researchers acquired access to each of the participant's health records and tracked the number of times they visited the doctor both before and after the study.

Because all the participants were college students of average health, the number of doctor visits by participants in both the control group and the Expressive Writing group should have been approximately the same. However, over the subsequent weeks and months, students who had written about traumatic experiences made 43% fewer visits to the doctor than those who wrote about superficial topics. Writing about personal trauma led the research subjects to seek medical attention at roughly half the rate of the control group (Pennebaker & Evans, 2014, pp. 4–8).

This study inspired other researchers. In the years since, over 300 studies have been published on the benefits of Expressive Writing. As the data poured in, it became clear that Expressive Writing could be used to mitigate the detrimental health effects of traumatic experiences.

Through these studies, we've learned that Expressive Writing about a traumatic experience has a positive effect on the immune system and helps patients with chronic health problems. Patients suffering from asthma, arthritis, AIDS, cancer, irritable bowel syndrome, high blood pressure, and lupus have all shown improvement after writing about a traumatic experience. Multiple studies have shown that people who engage in Expressive Writing experience long-term better moods, less depression and anxiety, and improved cognitive function. College-student participants in various studies earned higher grades in subsequent semesters. Studies in which participants were asked to wear a small tape recorder found that subjects laughed more easily and more often and used more positive-emotion words in the weeks and months after doing Expressive Writing (Pennebaker & Evans, 2014, pp. 9–13).

By writing about a traumatic experience, participants were engaged in a process of revising their story about that event. They were using their adult, best self perspective to recast that story with fresh eyes. From a mature perspective, they could revise the childmind's story into a truer story that released them from the hurtspot, leaving them healthier, more relaxed, and more effective in their lives. When a hurtspot story releases, it frees up energy that the body can use for better health.

## The Original Four-Day Pennebaker Expressive Writing Method

The following approach is the most rigorously tested Expressive Writing method for helping people heal from the effects of traumatic experiences. When leading a four-day or longer training with educators, this is the approach I use.

The process entails participants writing for 20 minutes a day on four consecutive days about a particular troubling or traumatic experience. Though the instructions are specific, once they are given, participants are free to go wherever the writing takes them. Here are the instructions:

1.  Think of a past traumatic experience or emotional upheaval that has been influencing your life. It's best to choose an experience you have a little distance from rather than trying to write about a recent event. You will be writing about your deepest thoughts and feelings about that traumatic experience. In your writing, let go and explore this event and how it has affected you.
2.  If a particular topic seems like too much to handle, save that topic for another day. Write about something else.
3.  Write continuously for 20 minutes a day on four consecutive days. Write without concern for spelling or grammar. If you run out of things to say, simply repeat what you've already written.
4.  As you write, relate this experience to other parts of your life, such as your job or your relationships. Consider how the event relates to who you have been in the past, who you will likely be in the future, and who you are now.

5. Rather than recounting the experience, reconstrue it, explain it. Consider the motivations, thoughts, and feelings of each party involved.

On the second day, follow the previous day's instructions, but now go even deeper into your thoughts and feelings about the event, how it is affecting your work, your relationships, and how you see yourself.

On the third day, continue writing about your deepest thoughts and feelings concerning the event without repeating what you have already written. Instead, explore the traumatic experience from different perspectives and in different ways. Also, wonder how this event has shaped your life, exploring how it may have made you both stronger and more vulnerable.

On the fourth day, continue to explore your deepest thoughts and feelings about the traumatic event, but also stand back and think about the experience more broadly. Consider anything you haven't yet confronted. At this stage of the process, shift your focus toward what you have learned, lost, and gained from this upheaval. Also, wonder how you can use the experience to guide your thoughts and actions in the future. Your main focus on the fourth day is to turn the entire experience into a meaningful story you can take with you into the future.

At the end of each day's writing session, Pennebaker and his team had participants complete the following brief questionnaire:

Put a number between 0 and 10 by each question where 0 is "not at all" and 10 is "a great deal."

\_\_\_\_ A. To what degree did you express your deepest thoughts and feelings?

\_\_\_\_ B. To what degree do you currently feel sad or upset?

\_\_\_\_ C. To what degree do you currently feel happy?

\_\_\_\_ D. To what degree was today's writing valuable and meaningful for you?

E. Briefly describe how your writing went today so you
may refer to this later.

(Pennebaker & Evans, 2014, pp. 31–41)

When I introduce Expressive Writing in a workshop, participants are often curious if some approaches to the process are more
effective than others. Research offers a few hints in this regard.
One is that the people who benefit most from the process use their
writing time to construct a coherent and meaningful story that
moves toward resolution (Pennebaker & Smyth, 2016, p. 153).
The construction of this story typically evolves over the course of
the four days, with many participants reporting that what they
wrote on the first day came out in a disorganized jumble, but by
the fourth day, they had turned their traumatic experience into a
coherent, knowledge-informed story that allowed them to let go
of the trauma derived story.

Research also indicates that Expressive Writing yields excellent results when participants shift perspectives in their writing.
In analyzing three Expressive Writing studies, researchers found
that the more frequently people oscillated their use of pronouns
between first-person singular (I, me, my) and all other pronouns
(such as we, she, they), the greater the benefit they received
(Pennebaker & Chung, 2007). This finding suggests that shifting perspectives is effective in reframing stuck stories around
hurtspots. Although the evidence regarding shifting perspectives is strong, researchers caution that the shifts in perspective
may be the result of some underlying change, rather than the
cause (Pennebaker & Chung, 2007).

Still, shifting perspectives is an approach worthy of experimentation. When leading five-day teacher trainings, I often add
a fifth day of writing to Dr. Pennebaker's original four-day process. On that day, I ask participants to rewrite the story they've
been working on for four days, shifting the point of view to a
third-person omniscient perspective, where they view the story
from outside it, describing what happened, narrating their own
thoughts and feelings as a character in the story, while also
being able to access and write about the thoughts and feelings
of each of the other characters. Drawing from research that

points to the power of having a strength-based personal narrative (Cable, 2020), I suggest that participants construct a narrative of the event that depicts themselves as a heroic protagonist overcoming obstacles, using details that highlight their own strengths, goodness, and resilience. I invite them to show their hero coming out of the traumatic experience with new capacities, wisdom, or a new perspective, and to finish their story by describing where their hero or heroine is going from here. What will their protagonist do with what they've gained through this experience?

For participants who feel resistant to writing about the topic that most weighs on them, I offer two suggestions. First, they can write about a different experience, one they feel more confident to approach. A person's inner wisdom about their readiness to confront a particular traumatic experience can and should be trusted. Second, if the person still wants to write about that weighty event but feels daunted by it, they can adapt the process by writing a fictionalized version of their story. They can still express their thoughts and feelings about the traumatic event through fictionalized characters, settings, and scenes that represent their traumatic experience without writing out the specifics of their own ordeal. Participants who have taken this alternate approach report that it has worked well. It seems to yield as much benefit for them as the regular process does for the others.

Expressive Writing can be used to transmute hurtspots even when a person can't recall the specific traumatic experiences that engendered them. Because people are prone to repress memories of childhood trauma, it's not uncommon for a person to experience a hurtspot reaction but be unable to identify the traumatic experience from which it originated. Sometimes, they have a vague sense of something that happened over time, such as "my father was often critical of me," but have a hard time pinpointing a particular traumatic experience to write about.

In such cases, a hurtspot reaction can be used as a doorway to the underlying story that is holding them back. The person can write about the experience of a hurtspot reaction, their deepest thoughts and feelings that arise when the hurtspot is active in their system, and describe how the hurtspot has affected their life. Once they get into the writing, they will likely be able to identify other experiences, farther back in time, that stirred up similar feelings and similar thoughts about themselves. Writing about those experiences may lead them to recognize the story about themselves that keeps the hurtspot intact. Once they've identified the story and explored how it has affected them, they can find their way to construct a truer, more authentic story to put in its place.

With Expressive Writing, we can be our own researchers, adapting the process to what works best for us. Having done the four-day Expressive Writing process myself multiple times, now when I notice the pain of a hurtspot arising, it frequently requires only a single writing session for me to gain the perspective I need to release it.

To help you along on your Expressive Writing journey, here are two additional Expressive Writing processes from *Expressive Writing, Words that Heal* (Pennebaker & Evans, 2014). These are both single-session writes, making them useful for when time is short.

## Brief Perspective Switching

Write about a conflict, event, emotional upset, or other issue you've been dealing with. Because you will write about an experience from two points of view, for only 10 minutes each, it is recommended that you don't start with a major traumatic experience. Whatever experience you choose, write about the experience in two 10-minute sessions, taking a few minutes' break between each session.

1. Write about the event in first person, describing your emotions, thoughts, and reactions in response to the event (10 minutes).
2. Write about the event in third person. Look back at what you wrote in first person and rewrite it from a third-person perspective as if you are describing it from outside the story. Include much of the same content as in the

first-person writing but from this different perspective (10 minutes).

3. After writing, notice how writing in third person felt in comparison to writing in first person. What new perspectives might be available to you from the third-person view?

4. If you found the the third-person perspective useful, in your next writing session, you may want to try using it to address a more significant trauma or emotional upheaval. This time take the entire 20 minutes to continuously write about this traumatic event from a third-person perspective (Pennebaker & Evans, 2014, pp. 76–78).

## Experimenting with a Symbolic Audience

Another approach that can help dislodge a stuck story is writing to a series of imagined audiences. This approach can help us gain greater detachment from a difficult experience. Though some of these imagined audience members might be real people, we won't actually share the writing with them; the writing is for us. In this exercise, write about a difficult personal experience to four imaginary audiences, writing for five minutes to each one.

1. *Authority figure*: Imagine you are telling an authority figure about a traumatic experience in your life. This person may be a police officer, a boss, a teacher, a judge—someone with whom you have a formal relationship. The authority figure does not have to be part of the story. Tell this person about the event and describe your thoughts and feelings (both then and now) and how the experience has affected your life.

2. *A close friend*: Imagine you are telling a close, understanding friend about this experience, someone you deeply trust and who will accept you no matter what you say. Tell this person about the event and describe your thoughts and feelings (both then and now) and how the experience has affected your life.

3. *Another person involved in the traumatic experience*: Imagine that your writing will be evaluated by this other person, who has a different perspective on what happened and on what the experience meant. Tell this person about the event, and describe your thoughts and feelings (both then and now) and how the experience has affected your life.

4. *Yourself*: This time, you are the only audience. Tell yourself about the event and describe your thoughts and feelings (both then and now) and how the experience has affected your life.

> *Post-Writing Reflection*: Analyze how each description of the event differed. Did you feel different as you were writing them? Did some feel more genuine than others? Did writing to any of these audiences give you a different perspective on the experience?
>
> (Pennebaker & Evans, 2014, pp. 89–92)

One common concern people have about Expressive Writing is apprehension about doing the process right and following the instructions exactly. However, the benefits of Expressive Writing are available even when the instructions aren't explicitly followed. Dr. Pennebaker himself told me that his own approach to Expressive Writing has evolved toward "simply encouraging people to write about issues or events that were stressful, painful, or in some way weighed upon them." He has also found that when people are asked to write about a major life challenge, such as losing a job or receiving a diagnosis of a disease, many don't write about the assigned topic at all. They write about whatever is weighing on them at the time, and still receive great value from the process.

We can all use Expressive Writing to rewrite our old limiting stories and liberate ourselves from the tyranny of hurtspots, even if we don't think of ourselves as writers. Once we begin the process, we can trust the story-making part of our brain to take

over and, with the advantage that comes from maturity, construct a story informed by knowledge and perspective—a story
that will improve our ability to fulfill our inborn potential and
create a more resilient best self.

Although there is no wrong way to do Expressive Writing,
you will get better results if you set aside time for this process
and do it in a quiet setting without distraction. Then, as you
move through life in the following weeks and months, watch to
see if you've strengthened your capacity to retain your best self
in situations that, previously, could have prompted a hurtspot
reaction.

 **REFLECTION QUESTIONS**

*Grab a notebook and something to write with and respond to the
following questions:*

1   What is a traumatic event or a bothersome hurtspot you would
    like to explore more deeply through Expressive Writing?
2   Choose one of the processes described in this chapter. I rec-
    ommend starting with the original four-day Expressive Writing
    Process and completing all four days, with an optional fifth day
    to change the perspective to third-person point of view.
3   Complete whichever Expressive Writing process you've cho-
    sen. Describe any insights you've gained.

# 26

# The Liberating Power of Radical Acceptance

Hurtspots have two components: an injurious story generated during a traumatic experience, and unprocessed pain. This means there are two ways to heal a hurtspot. One way is through revising the story, which can be done in therapy or, as we saw in the previous chapter, through Expressive Writing. The other way is through addressing the unprocessed emotional pain. Radical acceptance offers us a doorway into the pain, allowing us to process it so we can release it.

In Chapter 11 we looked at how radical acceptance of our students can transform our experience of teaching while turning our classrooms into oases of acceptance and belonging. Now we will turn the power of radical acceptance on ourselves, transforming our inner landscape into an oasis of acceptance and belonging for us.

Radical acceptance has been used as a therapeutic approach for quite some time. In the 1970s, Marsha Linehan began experimenting with treatment of suicidal patients with borderline personality disorder and developed a therapeutic approach called dialectical behavior therapy (DBT). DBT is now the gold standard for treating people with borderline personality disorder (Greenstein, 2017). Further studies have shown DBT to be effective in treating other mental health issues, including PTSD, major depression, bipolar disorder, and eating disorders.

DOI: 10.4324/9781003360513-31

At the heart of DBT is the premise: the first step toward positive change is radical acceptance of oneself, one's emotions and thoughts, the world, and others just as they are. As Linehan says, "To change who/what you are, you must first accept who/what you are" (2021, p. 251).

Radical acceptance of oneself and one's emotional response is of particular importance when healing from the injurious effects of a traumatic experience. When a hurtspot is activated, we are inundated with a rush of unwanted thoughts, sensations, and emotions. Our natural response is to resist them—to numb ourselves, to push them away. But this is the opposite of what is necessary to process the pain and free ourselves from the debilitating effects of hurtspots. Instead of resisting, we need to "befriend the sensations" (Van der Kolk, 2014, p. 102). In other words, we need to learn to bring radical acceptance to the thoughts, emotions, and sensations set off by hurtspots.

I first discovered the utility of bringing radical acceptance to troublesome thoughts, emotional pain, and excruciating sensations in my body decades before I heard the term or understood what I was doing. I was in my twenties and consumed by chronic fatigue syndrome. Physically and emotionally, I was a mess. My then girlfriend, Laura, wanted a travel adventure. I sold roses door to door and saved money until, between the two of us, we had enough for an extended low-budget trip. We boarded a bus from Oregon to Brownsville, Texas, where we got off, walked across the border, and disappeared into Mexico. We traveled south on third-class buses and trains, ultimately ending up in Corozal, Belize, where we decided to stay for a while.

Corozal is a sleepy town right on the Caribbean Sea. In the afternoons, we'd swim in the warm, aquamarine water. Every morning, we'd take the short walk to the local tortilleria to buy fresh, still steaming tortillas. The cottage didn't have a stove, so we devised a makeshift barbecue from an old truck rim and a square of wire fencing over which we cooked our meals: mostly rice and beans, vegetables, and fried plantain. We'd fry any leftover tortillas in coconut oil to make our own corn chips sprinkled with sea salt. The weather was perpetually beautiful, with a fresh sea breeze coming off the Caribbean. It was perfect—and I was as unhappy as I'd ever been.

One day, while sitting on the bed, utterly depressed, mad, ashamed, and feeling sorry for myself, I was confronted by the unwelcome realization that *I had brought myself with me.* I had traveled 4,000 miles, and here I was, the same old miserable self I had hoped to leave behind in Oregon. In a moment of cheerless clarity, I saw that trying to run from myself had been wasted energy. All my attempts over the years to fix myself, distract myself, fight myself, escape myself, had done nothing but lead me exactly here, wretched and desolate.

There was nothing left to do but sit with the suffering—the despair, the brain fog, the lethargy, the leaden belly, the drowning sadness. I decided in that moment to surrender to it and simply feel what I felt. *Go ahead,* I said to whatever it was that felt so awful, *do your worst. I'll just sit here and take it.*

So I sat there. I watched as self-hating thoughts shot off like flares in my brain. *I am no good. Nothing I do will ever never be enough. I am a miserable disappointment. My illness is my fault. I am permanently broken.*

I opened myself to experiencing and accepting all of it, letting the anguish stream through. It felt like drowning in a personal hell. I sat like that for two days. I thought I was giving up, but really, I was setting myself up for a new start.

By the third day, a space in me had opened up. I awoke that morning feeling different, somewhat better. Then Laura walked in. "I want you to dig a well for me," she said.

While I had been sitting in my puddle of woe, she had been out talking to people about her dream of building a healing center. She met a local man who said he would sell her a five-acre plot of land on the outskirts of Corozal. "It was perfect," she told me. Though she hadn't signed any papers and there was no formal agreement, she wanted me to dig a well on that land the very next day.

Looking back, I would characterize our relationship as unhealthy. Laura was older, and I leaned on her pretty hard, depended on her, believed I needed her. She could be critical, and I would take it, thinking it was what I deserved.

Early the next morning, we went to a hardware store, bought a mattock, and made our way to the plot of land. It was all jungle, except for a small clearing, which is where she wanted me to dig. I began swinging the mattock. To my surprise, I had more energy than I'd had in a while. By afternoon I was in a hole up to my waist—deep enough that I couldn't get a good swing with the mattock without first widening the hole, so that's what I started to do. Laura saw what I was doing and said I was doing it wrong. She said she didn't want a wider hole; it needed to be a narrow hole. I explained that I couldn't keep it narrow with the tool I was using. Well, she said, other men could do it. Why couldn't I? "When I was in the Peace Corps in Mauritania," she added, "a man had dug a well for me, and it was a narrow hole."

This was the perfect snare for one of my hurtspots: I wasn't man enough. Other men were man enough. I wasn't. Ugly thoughts began churning in my head—defensive, angry, shame-based thoughts. I stood in the hole as the thoughts, feelings, and distressing sensations swirled through me, noticing and accepting them as I had been doing for the past few days. And then they dissolved. I heard the birds in the jungle canopy and saw them flitting in the branches. The shadows cast by the leaves were gently moving. I took a deep breath, inhaling the scent of the freshly turned soil.

Like a man awakening from a trance, I looked up and saw Laura scowling at the edge of the hole. I didn't feel angry. I didn't feel defensive. I just felt clear. For the first time, it didn't matter what she thought of me.

I climbed out of the hole, handed her the mattock, and calmly said, "Tomorrow morning I'm leaving. I am going to Guatemala."

The next morning, we hugged goodbye and I stepped on a bus to Antigua, Guatemala. Only a few days earlier, I believed the untrue story that I couldn't manage without her. By bringing radical acceptance to the emotional and physical pain of a hurtspot, something in me released. As the bus pulled away, I opened my window and watched the jungle pass by. Instead of feeling trepidation, I felt joy.

I still had a long way to go when it came to healing hurtspots, but I had begun. That start sent me on my own adventure to

Guatemala and ultimately to meeting Paul Richards, learning karate, and becoming a teacher. Through radical acceptance, I had stepped out of a hurtspot trap and set my life in a new direction.

Those unhappy days in Belize demonstrated that there is value in sitting with discomfort. Although doing so can feel like helplessly falling through darkness with nothing to catch us, radical acceptance can make it a passage to a healthier version of ourselves.

Nonacceptance lies at the heart of every hurtspot story. Bessel van der Kolk says, "If you were abused as a child, you are likely to have a childlike part living inside you that is frozen in time, still holding fast to this kind of self-loathing and denial" (2014, p. 281). To heal, we need to bring radical acceptance to that childlike part and what it is feeling. Just as a teacher bringing radical acceptance to her students can transform a disparate group of unruly individuals into a learning community, so bringing radical acceptance to the parts of ourselves that are suffering turn our internal village into a healthy community. The hurtful untrue stories we tell ourselves about ourselves crumble in the light of radical self-acceptance.

With radical acceptance, I was able to stand in that hole and watch the hurtful thoughts without believing them. Later, I learned that whenever life hurled me into a hurtspot reaction, I could combine both radical acceptance and Expressive Writing to both revise the story and process the unprocessed pain.

Often, hurtspots get triggered at inconvenient times, maybe while teaching a class. In such situations, it is tempting to repress the thoughts, emotions, and sensations that arise, to pretend we are fine, to try to override what is actually happening in our body and mind. But for the sake of ourselves and our students, it is much better for us to be easy on ourselves, keeping our heart open and bringing radical acceptance to the arising thoughts and feelings without believing them to be true indicators of the situation or of who we are and what we can do.

When I am overcome by a hurtspot reaction while in front of a class and a critical thought about myself arises, I remember *uke* and receive that thought. In my own mind, I respond: *Maybe that critical thought about me is true, but more likely, it's a hurt part of me reaching out for acceptance. In fact, I don't really know who I am or what I'm capable of.* And then from this soft, accepting space, while allowing the changing stream of experience to move through me, I teach.

Strangely, the days when I've been triggered into a hurtspot reaction and have brought radical acceptance to myself have been some of my best days in the classroom.

Self-acceptance frees us from the trance of unworthiness, from the ongoing sense that we aren't doing enough and, to become a good enough teacher, we should try harder. It helps us remember that our best self isn't the self we bring just when we're unbothered and content. It is also there for us to embody when we're hurting or grieving or feeling despair. Radical acceptance provides the space to find our *Yes* for ourselves, exactly as we are. Our best self won't be perfect; we will still make mistakes. Yet laden as it is with foibles, limitations, and its messy magnificence, we can trust it. Our best self is the best self we have, and it's enough.

 **REFLECTION QUESTION**

*Grab a notebook and something to write with and respond to the following questions:*

1. Think of something about yourself and your experience that you notice yourself having an automatic resistance toward. Sit with that and breathe, bringing curiosity to what it would mean for you to accept that part of yourself, or that difficult experience.

# Conclusion

## A New Direction Forward

I'm writing this conclusion while sitting in a coffee shop on one of the last shimmering days of summer. Next week I will be back in my classroom. For many teachers, the past school year was the most difficult of their career. From where I stand, it doesn't look like this year, or the year after, will be much better. The news headlines are calling the current teacher shortage catastrophic. Teachers are exhausted, feeling unappreciated, even disrespected by major segments of society. Education is at the center of a bitter culture war; states are passing laws that constrain teachers, while partisan interests misrepresent educators and pit parents against them. This is no way to run an education system, no way to take care of our children and their teachers. And yet, teachers give me hope.

As I lead teachers through Teach from Your Best Self trainings, I am heartened by their strength, their dedication for students, their resilience. These teachers see the truth of the brokenness of education and still courageously show up to teach our kids day after day.

At the same time, I'm also aware that helping teachers thrive in an unhealthy system isn't a long-term solution to what ails education. The system needs to change.

The approaches that I recommend for teachers in the classroom offer clues about how we can reform education. Each of the approaches in this book can be applied on school-wide, district-wide, and education-system-wide scales. Instead of tolerating an education system built on pressure, control, and burdening teachers with more to do, the well-being of students, staff, and district employees would be protected. *In shin tonkei*— high-impact/low-effort teaching—would be a guiding principle.

DOI: 10.4324/9781003360513-32

Policies, norms, and procedures would be reevaluated with ROI in mind. Tasks and duties that offer low ROI would be taken off teachers' plates. Teachers would be set up to succeed. The Best Self Model for School Reform points the way toward an education system that is good for students and educators alike.

In this model, school and district leadership prioritize supporting the best selves of their staff. As in the classroom-scale Best Self Model for Teaching and Learning in Chapter 8, each of the three elements in the Best Self Model for School Reform synergistically reinforces and amplifies the other two in a positive feedback loop. For policymakers who see the relationship between a teacher's best self and a student's success, this model offers a direction toward sustainable education reform. It prompts a big question: what might an education system look like that purposefully takes care of its teachers?

Teachers want to bring their best. Effective education reform would mean changing the system so it supports teachers to do that, ultimately empowering educators to finally fulfill the promise of what a system devoted to the growth and learning of young people could be.

Teaching may be the hardest job there is. Yet, I also think teaching may be the best job there is. Education is where futures

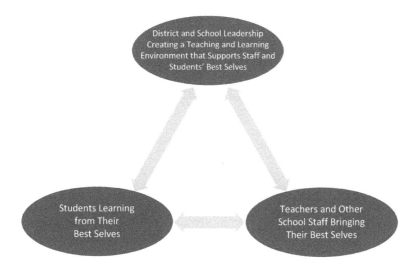

**FIGURE C.1** The Best Self Model of School Reform

are made, where young people are midwifed into realizing who they are and what they are capable of.

We can be the inspired, fiercely *Yes*-based teachers who emerge from the stress and pressure of today's teaching conditions with new strengths, to rewrite the story of education. We can meet difficulty and transform it into triumph. Of course we can; we're teachers. It's what we do.

 **REFLECTION QUESTIONS**

*Grab a notebook and something to write with and respond to the following questions:*

1 Make a list of the skills, principles, and practices from this book that you can see yourself applying right away.
2 Moving forward, what will be your first steps to make teaching more sustainable for you?

# Acknowledgments

The fact that this book exists is something of a miracle, one that could have occurred only through the support of an amazing group of people.

First, I want to thank the following stellar educators who, despite the pressures of their jobs, made time to be beta readers, graciously reading an early draft and offering feedback as I figured out how to shape the message: Amanda Elliot, Nathan Breeden, Amy Sayre, Lisa North, Jureen Gardner, Emily Brink, Julia Cuppy, Camille Schuler, Kari Miller, Josh Ingram, Haley Martin-Sherman, Lisa Yamashita, and Tisha Richmond. An additional thanks to educator-author Tisha Richmond for inspiring me that teachers can be authors and for helping me set up a Twitter account (yes, I needed help with that).

I am grateful to my good friend, fellow author, and karateka Richard Seidman for providing helpful feedback on the first several chapters, as well as my dear friend Gitanjali Nandan for doing the same.

Thank you to Lauren Davis, education publisher at Routledge, for seeing the potential in this book and warmly agreeing to help bring it to life, and to the rest of the Routledge team who have expertly brought this book to publication.

I owe a debt of gratitude to my friend and editor Carolyn Bond, who brought her editing genius to bear on this book. Carolyn never wavered from letting me know when the writing was wordy, overblown, weak, or unclear, consistently pointing me toward clear, crisp prose. Carolyn, I know the reader thanks you as well.

I can't say enough about the community of educators I have gotten to work with through Teach from Your Best Self workshops and trainings. You have been an invaluable source of positive messages for me. I don't think I could have sustained full-time teaching and leading Teach from Your Best Self work-shops while also writing this book without your love and support.

In regard to the Teach from Your Best Self trainings, I want to thank Heidi Olivadoti and the folks over at the Southern Oregon Regional Educator Network for their generous support to help me launch this work.

Sometimes we get to work with someone who, with ease and grace, consistently brings out our best. In this regard, work-ing with Margaret Perrow, professor and Director of the Oregon Writing Project at Southern Oregon University, has been one of the great privileges of my life. Thank you, Margaret, for reading an early draft, offering feedback to make it better, and then part-nering with me to write grants and organize Teach from Your Best Self workshops for educators. Most of all, I want to thank you for the precious gift of believing in me.

Karate plays a significant role in this book, and none of that would be possible without the attention and tutelage of Sensei Aaron Ortega, who took this inept beginner and skillfully men-tored him to black belt.

The sensei-student relationship is a sacred one, and I am deeply grateful for the guidance I ongoingly receive from Grandmaster Tom Spellman, the model warrior-scholar, who has helped me see that traditional karate isn't just about punch-ing and kicking; it is a path of integration and awakening on the way to freedom.

Without Paul Richards's mentorship neither the book nor I as the teacher who could write it would have been possible. By sharing his body of work through the Sente Center, Paul intro-duced me to many of the concepts contained in this book. These include: the importance of presence and state of being, the idea of a person as a village of aspects with a genuine nature under-lying it, the application of ROI to life, *Yes* and saying *No* from *Yes*, the advantage of having a preeminent *Yes*, deploying atten-tion as a field, relating to attention as a form of nourishment, and the importance of positive messages. Paul and his amazing wife, Patty, have shown me that growth and change are always available and that every moment holds hidden advantages, just waiting to be tapped. Paul and Patty, I thank you from the bottom of my heart.

Finally, I want to thank my badass wife, Judy. As the best natural teacher I know, you inspire me. Thank you for not letting our world fall apart while I holed up in the cave of my office to work on this book, and thank you for not murdering me for the extra slack you had to pick up. You stood by my side, reading chapters, offering wise feedback, and propping me up when I slumped. Most important, I thank you for your continual flow of hilarious and irreverent comments that kept me from taking myself too seriously. Seriously, I adore you.

# References

Aguilar, E. (2018). *Onward: Cultivating Emotional Resilience in Educators*. John Wiley & Sons.

Allegeretto, S., & Mishel, L. (2020, September 17). Teacher Pay Penalty Dips but Persists in 2019. *Economic Policy Institute*. https://www.epi.org/publication/teacher-pay-penalty-dips-but-persists-in-2019-public-school-teachers-earn-about-20-less-in-weekly-wages-than-nonteacher-college-graduates/

Arnsten, A., Mazure, C. M., & Sinha, R. (2021). This Is Your Brain in Meltdown. *Scientific American*, 30(2), 12–17.

Blair, C. (2012). Treating a Toxin to Learning. *Scientific American Mind*, 23(4), 64–67. https://doi.org/10.1038/scientificamericanmind0912-64

Cable, D. M. (2019). *Alive at Work, The Neuroscience of Helping Your People Love What They Do*. Harvard Business Review Press.

Cable, D. M. (2020). *Exceptional: Build Your Personal Highlight Reel and Unlock Your Potential*. Chronicle Prism.

Covey, S. (1989). *The Seven Habits of Highly Effective People*. Simon and Schuster.

Danziger, S., Levav, J., & Avnaim-Pesso, L. (2011). Extraneous Factors in Judicial Decisions. *Proceedings of the National Academy of Sciences*, 108(17), 6889–6892. https://doi.org/10.1073/pnas.1018033108

*Directed Attention Fatigue—Wikidoc*. (n.d.). https://www.wikidoc.org/index.php/Directed_attention_fatigue

Eurich, T. (2018, January 4). What Self-Awareness Really Is (and How to Cultivate It). *Harvard Business Review*. https://hbr.org/2018/01/what-self-awareness-really-is-and-how-to-cultivate-it

Fay Greene, M. (2020, July/August). Can an Unloved Child Learn to Love? *The Atlantic*, 326(1), 64–75.

Felitti V. J. (2002). The Relation Between Adverse Childhood Experiences and Adult Health: Turning Gold into Lead. *The Permanente Journal*, *6*(1), 44–47. https://doi.org/10.7812/TPP/02.994

Garcia Cerdán, A. (2017, June 8). *Mirror Neurons: The Most Powerful Learning Tool*. Cognifit. https://blog.cognifit.com/mirror-neurons/

Garcia, E., & Weiss, E. (2019, March 26). *The Teacher Shortage Is Real, Large and Growing, and Worse Than We Thought. Economic Policy Institute*. https://www.epi.org/publication/the-teacher-shortage-is-real-large-and-growing-and-worse-than-we-thought-the-first-report-in-the-perfect-storm-in-the-teacher-labor-market-series/

Glasser, W. (1990). *The Quality School: Managing Students Without Coercion*. Harper Collins.

Golden, C. (1998). America's Graduation from High School: The Evolution and Spread of Secondary Schooling in the Twentieth Century. *Journal of Economic History*, *58*(2), 345–374.

Greenstein, L. (2017, June 7). Treating Borderline Personality Disorder. *National Alliance on Mental Illness*.

Hamilton, J. (2014, February 24). Orphans' Lonely Beginnings Reveal How Parents Shape a Child's Brain. *NPR.org*. https://www.npr.org/sections/health-shots/2014/02/20/280237833/orphans-lonely-beginnings-reveal-how-parents-shape-a-childs-brain

Hammond, Z. L. (2015). *Culturally Responsive Teaching and The Brain: Promoting Authentic Engagement and Rigor Among Culturally and Linguistically Diverse Students*. Corwin.

Heckman, J. J., & LaFontaine, P. A. (2010). The American High School Graduation Rate: Trends and Levels. *The Review of Economics and Statistics*, *92*,(2), 244–262. https://doi.org/10.1162/rest.2010.12366

Heissel, J., Levy, D., & Adam, E. (2017, June 9). Stress, Sleep, and Performance on Standardized Tests: Understudied Pathways to the Achievement Gap. *American Educational Research Association*, *3*(3), 1–17. https://doi.org/10.1177%2F2332858417713488

Huberman, A. (2021). Secrets to Surviving Stress. *Scientific American*, *30*(2), 60–61.

Hyams, J. (1979). *Zen in the Martial Arts*. Bantam Books.

Kaplan, S., & Berman, M. G. (2010). Directed Attention as a Common Resource for Executive Functioning and Self-Regulation. *Perspectives on Psychological Science*, 5(1), 43–57. https://doi.org/10.1177/1745691609356784

Klusmann, U., Ludtke, O., & Richter, D. (2016). Teachers' Emotional Exhaustion Is Negatively Related to Students' Achievement: Evidence from a Large-Scale Assessment Study. *Journal of Educational Psychology*, 108(8), 1193–1203.

Levitin, D. J. (2015, March 11). *Why the Modern World Is Bad for Your Brain*. Wu Tsai Neurosciences Institute. https://neuroscience.stanford.edu/news/why-modern-world-bad-your-brain

Lewis, E. (2019, August 22). *Adverse Childhood Experiences and the Developing Brain*. National Center for Mental Health. https://www.ncmh.info/2019/08/22/adverse-childhood-experiences-and-the-developing-brain/

Lieberman, M. (2021, October 15). How Staff Shortages Are Crushing Schools. *Education Week*. https://www.edweek.org/leadership/how-staff-shortages-are-crushing-schools/2021/10

Linehan, M. M. (2021). *Building a Life Worth Living: A Memoir*. Random House Publishing Group.

Marken, S., & Agrawal, S. (2022, June 13). K-12 Workers Have Highest Burnout Rate in U.S. *Gallup News*. https://news.gallup.com/poll/393500/workers-highest-burnout-rate.aspx

Meckler, L. (2022, January 30). Public Education Is Facing a Crisis of Epic Proportions. *The Washington Post*. https://www.washingtonpost.com/education/2022/01/30/public-education-crisis-enrollment-violence/

*Mental Health Impact of the COVID-19 Pandemic on Teachers and Parents of K-12 Students*. (2021). CDC Foundation. https://www.cdcfoundation.org/mental-health-triangulated-report?inline

National Assessment of Educational Progress. (2019). "Negativity Bias" in Risk for Depression and Anxiety: Brain–Body Fear

Circuitry Correlates, 5-HTT-LPR, and Early Life Stress [exam results]. *Neuroimage*, *47*(3), 804–814.

Oyserman, D., Bybee, D., & Terry, K. (2006). Possible Selves and Academic Outcomes: How and When Possible Selves Impel Action. *Journal of Personality and Social Psychology*, *91*(1), 188–204. https://doi.org/10.1037/0022-3514.91.1.188

Pennebaker, J. W., & Chung, C. K. (2007). Expressive Writing, Emotional Upheavals, and Health. In H. S. Friedman & R. C. Silver (Eds.), *Foundations of Health Psychology* (pp. 263–284). Oxford University Press.

Pennebaker, J. W., & Evans, J. F. (2014). *Expressive Writing: Words that Heal*. Idyll Arbor, Inc.

Pennebaker, J. W., & Smyth, J. M. (2016). *Opening Up by Writing It Down: How Expressive Writing Improves Health and Eases Emotional Pain* (Third). The Guilford Press.

Perna, M. (2022, January 4). Why Education Is About to Reach a Crisis of Epic Proportions. *Forbes*. https://www.forbes.com/sites/markcperna/2022/01/04/why-education-is-about-to-reach-a-crisis-of-epic-proportions/?sh=7bfc20ff78c7

*Richard Ingersoll Updates Landmark Study of the American Teaching Force, Now Covering 3 Decades* [press release]. (2018, October 23). University of Pennsylvania Graduate School of Education. https://www.gse.upenn.edu/news/press-releases/richard-ingersoll-updates-landmark-study-american-teaching-force-now-covering-3

*Road Rage: How to Avoid Aggressive Driving*. (2013). AAA Foundation for Traffic Safety, Brochure. https://exchange.aaa.com/wp-content/uploads/2013/06/Road-Rage-Brochure.pdf

Ronfeldt, M., Loeb, S., & Wyckoff, J. (2013). *How Teacher Turnover Harms Student Achievement*. Stanford Center for Education Policy Analysis. https://cepa.stanford.edu/sites/default/files/TchTrnStAch%20AERJ%20RR%20not%20blind.pdf

Sapolsky, R. (2021). The Health-Wealth Gap. *Scientific America*, *30*(2), 48–53.

Southwick, S. M., & Charney, D. S. (2018). *Resilience: The Science of Mastering Life's Greatest Challenges*. Cambridge University Press.

Thoughtful Learning. (n.d.). *What Are the Social and Emotional Needs of the Brain?* https://k12.thoughtfullearning.com/FAQ/what-are-social-and-emotional-needs-brain

Tierney, J. (2011, August 17). Do You Suffer From Decision Fatigue? *The New York Times Magazine.* https://www.nytimes.com/2011/08/21/magazine/do-you-suffer-from-decision-fatigue.html

*U.S. High School Graduation Rates.* (n.d.). Randy Sprick's Safe & Civil Schools. https://www.safeandcivilschools.com/research/graduation_rates.php

Van der Kolk, B. (2014). *The Body Keeps the Score: Brain, Mind, and Body in the Healing of Trauma* (Reprint). Penguin Publishing Group.

Vestal, C. (2021, November 8). *COVID Harmed Kids' Mental Health—And Schools are Feeling It.* The PEW Charitable Trusts. https://www.pewtrusts.org/en/research-and-analysis/blogs/stateline/2021/11/08/covid-harmed-kids-mental-health-and-schools-are-feeling-it

Villarica, H. (2012, April 9). The Chocolate-and-Radish Experiment That Birthed the Modern Conception of Willpower. *The Atlantic.* https://www.theatlantic.com/health/archive/2012/04/the-chocolate-and-radish-experiment-that-birthed-the-modern-conception-of-willpower/255544/

Walker, T. (2022, February 1). Survey: Alarming Number of Educators May Soon Leave the Profession. *National Educational Association News.* https://www.nea.org/advocating-for-change/new-from-nea/survey-alarming-number-educators-may-soon-leave-profession

Weir, K. (2014). The lasting impact of neglect. *PsycEXTRA Dataset.* https://doi.org/10.1037/e515152014-014

*What's the Cost of Teacher Turnover.* (2017, September 13). The Learning Policy Institute. https://learningpolicyinstitute.org/product/the-cost-of-teacher-turnover

Whitman, W. (1855). Song of Myself, 52. *Leaves of Grass.*

Williams, L. M., Gatt, J. M., Schofield, P. R., Olivieri, G., Peduto, A., & Gordon, E. (2009). 'Negativity bias' in risk for depression and anxiety: Brain–body fear circuitry correlates, 5-HTT-LPR, and early life stress. *Neuroimage, 47*(3), 804–814.